Scroll Saw Handbook
with Patterns

Patrick Spielman

Sterling Publishing Co., Inc.   New York

Library of Congress Cataloging-in-Publication Data

Spielman, Patrick E.
    Scroll saw handbook with patterns / Patrick Spielman. — Special
ed.
        p.   cm.
    Includes index.
    ISBN 0-8069-6872-9 (pbk.)
    1. Jig saws. 2. Woodwork.   I. Title.
TT186.S673 1988
684'.083—dc19   88-24772
                                                       CIP

Special edition
Copyright © 1988 by Patrick and Patricia Spielman
Published by Sterling Publishing Co., Inc.
Two Park Avenue, New York, N.Y. 10016
The material in this book was
originally published by Sterling Publishing Co., Inc.,
under the titles "Scroll Saw Handbook" © 1986
by Patrick Spielman and "Scroll
Saw Pattern Book" © 1986 by Patrick
and Patricia Spielman
Manufactured in the United States of America
All rights reserved

Table of Contents

PREFACE

For the purposes of this book, the terms "scroll saw" and "jigsaw" have essentially the same meanings. The majority of manufacturers today call their machines scroll saws, and *Webster's New International Dictionary* (second edition) defines a scroll saw as "a ribbonlike saw stretched in a frame, adapted for sawing curved outlines . . ." Some of the new manufacturers of scroll saws do refer to the design of older-style, rigid-arm machines as jigsaws. Regardless of their preferences, for consistency all sawing machines discussed will be called scroll saws.

The scroll saws that have become available in recent years are simply fantastic machines. They should probably carry warning labels like: "Use of this machine could become addictive." The more you use a scroll saw, the more you want to use it, and the more you find to do with it. This is because scroll-sawing today is exciting, relaxing, and often very therapeutic. The scroll saw user's confidence and skills grow quickly with each new project. The intoxicating aroma of freshly cut wood, the quickness and high quality of cut, and the pure joy and satisfaction of working with scroll saws has captured the fancy of amateur, veteran, and professional woodcrafters alike. Men, women and children from ages 10 to 100 can become very skilled in a short time. One manufacturer estimates that 25 to 35 percent of all total sales is to women. Scroll-sawing has even become a "family experience" in many households.

SCROLL SAW FUNDAMENTALS

1

THE SCROLL SAW

Man's effort to substitute energy other than his own muscle power for sawing wood dates back before the discovery of America. Early saw mills were powered by animals, wind, and water.

Between 1600 and 1620, the first American saw mills appeared in Maine and Virginia. Some of the saws that cut logs into lumber had long blades rigged in a frame; these blades were spaced to cut boards of equal width. The saws moved up and down in a reciprocating action, and the cut was made only on the downward stroke of the saw. This reciprocating blade movement is the same basic cutting action incorporated in all scroll saws today.

The first scroll saws were handmade wood parts, except for a crude metal blade. The blade was strained or tensioned by attaching one end to a flexible wooden rod (used as a spring) that was attached to the shop ceiling. The blade extended downwards through the table, with the lower end connected to a foot treadle near the floor. (See Illus. 1.) The operator depressed the treadle to pull the blade downwards for the cutting stroke. The wooden spring rod raised the blade again when the foot pressure was released.

It is believed that the first fine scroll saw blades were invented by a German clockmaker in the late 1500s. Until the advent of the machine age, narrow-cutting blades were held in frames similar to the coping or fret saw frames still available today that are used for hand-sawing.

Illus. 1. *The earliest forms of scroll saws employed a reciprocating cutting action produced by a foot treadle. The blade was tensioned by a wooden spring rod attached to the ceiling.*

Scroll-sawing machines made with metal parts first appeared in the mid-1800s. They were moved up and down by a foot-powered treadle or pedal mechanism. The use of cast iron in the manufacture of scroll saws and other woodworking machines provided the necessary weight and rigidity. (See Illus. 2–4.)

No. 1 Amateur Saw.

Complete with Borer,   - $10.00
Without Borer,   -   -   -   8.00

This machine will cut pine of any thickness up to 1½ inches, and harder woods of proportionate thicknesses. It admits a swing of 18 inches around the blade, and accomplishes every branch of sawing within the range of general amateur work.

The table does not tilt, but sawing for inlay work can be done by placing a beveled strip under the stuff being sawed.

The price of the machine complete is **$10.00**.

The price of the machine without Boring Attachment is **$8.00**.

It weighs 40 pounds.

Boxed ready for shipment it weighs 63 pounds.

Illus. 2. This reprint from the 1907 W.F. & John Barnes Catalog shows an early scroll saw probably designed for the home workshop.

Illus. 3. A saw developed for professional, non-factory use featured larger cutting capacities.

No. 7 Scroll Saw Improved
Price $15.00

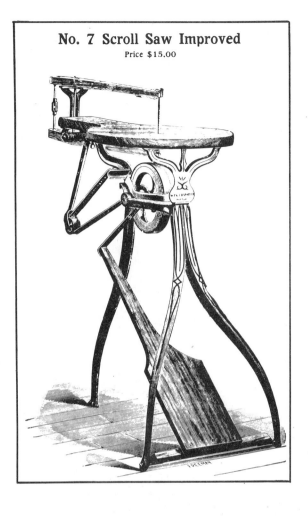

Scroll Saw No. 7
Price $15.00

This machine is designed for practical service in the workshops of carpenters and builders, cabinet makers and other wood workers.

WARRANTY

We warrant it to be well made, of good material and workmanship, and with reasonable practice to saw at the following rates: Pine, 2 inches thick, 1 foot per minute; 1 inch thick, 4 feet per minute; walnut, 3 inches thick, ½ foot per minute; 1 inch thick, 2 feet per minute, and other woods and thicknesses at proportionate rates.

The ordinary rate of speed when sawing is from 800 to 1200 strokes per minute. The saw leaves the work as smooth as is possible for any saw to do, and can be taken out and replaced in an instant for inside work.

The swing around the blade under the arm is 24 inches.
The length of the blade is 7 inches.
The table and arms are made of hard maple.
The frame is made of cast iron, strong, yet light.
The balance wheel runs on a steel arbor.
The machine weighs 60 pounds.
Boxed for shipment, 95 pounds.
We include one dozen blades with each machine.

The above cut shows our No. 7 Scroll Saw arranged with a countershaft. The price of countershaft, including the connecting band wheel on the machine, is $10.00. The price of No. 7 Scroll Saw, arranged with countershaft only (no foot power), is $20.00.
Speed of countershaft 500 R. P. M.
Tight and loose pulleys 4 in. diameter x 2 in. face.

Illus. 4. This factory scroll saw was belt-driven from the line shaft.

Early factories powered their machines from water wheels through long line shafts. The line shaft usually extended throughout the total length of the plant along the ceiling or floor. Each individual machine in the factory was belt-driven from that one line shaft. (See Illus. 4.) This system continued until electric power was introduced. However, many factories continued to employ the line shaft until the mid-1930s, even though small electric motors became available in the early 1900s.

Although cast iron was used for many parts on the earlier scroll saws, the flexing quality of wood remained essential to the design and function of the early constant-tension-saw frame arms. Almost all early manufacturers of scroll saws used hardwood for the arms and worktables.

One company that probably was the

largest manufacturer of scroll saws in the 1800s was the W. F. and John Barnes Company located in Rockford, Illinois, which manufactured a complete line of "Patent Foot and Hand Power Wood Working Machinery." Their line included many different scroll saws, and even circular saws and wood turning lathes that were efficiently foot-powered.

Some selected pages from the 1907 Barnes Company Catalog (No. 67) are shown in Illus. 2 – 4. Note their prices and their designs, which are in some cases similar to the constant-tension saws that are so popular now.

HOW SCROLL SAWS WORK

All scroll saws must have some way of converting the rotary motion of the motor to an up-and-down reciprocating action. (See Illus. 5.) Scroll saws are designed so the blade cuts on the downwards movement, so the teeth of the blade should always point downwards. How fast the blade goes up and down is specified as the strokes per minute (spm) or the cutting strokes per minute. The speed can vary from machine to machine. It depends upon the speed of the motor, which is specified as revolutions per minute (rpm). If a scroll saw is direct-drive type, which many are (it's the most basic), then the cutting strokes per minute will equal the revolutions per minute or speed of the motor. Sometimes it is better to change or slow down the cutting speed, particularly when sawing metal, plastic, or very thin material such as veneer.

Saws having speeds different from the speed of their drive motors are either belted-drive systems or variable-speed controlled saws. A belted-drive saw makes use of a combination of different size pulleys that are fitted on to the drive shaft and/or to the motor shaft. A belted-drive system is simple in design. It is easy to maintain and provides precise control of specific speeds.

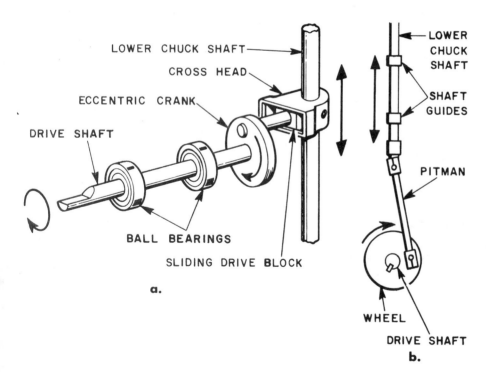

Illus. 5. Conventional methods of converting rotary motion into reciprocating motion: (a) eccentric crank on the left, and (b) the wheel and the pitman drive.

A mechanical means of actually changing the pulley sizes (diameters) with a single control crank while the saw is running is one form of a variable-speed saw. The motor speed does not change, but the spm does. This type of variable speed is found on the older, heavier, rigid-arm machines, such as the Delta and Powermatic. The other variable-speed system is activated electronically inside the motor, and actually slows or speeds up the rotation (rpm) of the motor shaft simply by the turn of a hand dial. Generally, the higher speeds are preferred for almost all wood-cutting jobs except sawing thin veneers.

The length of the cutting stroke equals the vertical distance travelled by the blade in one complete stroke. Stroke lengths vary from approximately ⅜ to 1⅛ inches, with a range of ¾ to 1 inch being the most common. Short-cutting strokes reduce saw efficiency and cutting speed when sawing medium to thick stock. Consequently, the longer strokes are usually preferred, but only if the mechanics of the saw provide proper vertical travel of the blade or proper tension throughout the stroke. Few saws available today have a provision for changing to a shorter stroke length. A shorter stroke length provides a higher degree of accuracy; this is beneficial when production-cutting thin materials such as metals, veneer, etc.

The throat of a scroll saw is that horizontal distance from the blade to the rear or vertical part of the saw frame. Throat capacities range from 12 to 26 inches, and again the middle range of 14 to 18 inches appears to be the most popular.

The depth of cut is the thickest piece of wood that can be "potentially" cut on a saw. Remember, hardwoods and softwoods cut a lot differently. You may be able to cut 2-inch oak, but how long will it take to complete the cut and what will be the quality of the cut? Will it be rough, smooth, or burned? Will it be straight with the cut edges flat and true, or will the cut surfaces bulge or slant and be out of square? (See Illus. 6.)

Illus. 6. The quality and trueness of cut are important, especially in thick stock. This 1½-inch pine should have a square edge. What will happen when thick hardwood is cut on the same saw?

BASIC SCROLL SAW DESIGNS

The styles or designs of scroll saws today fall into two distinct groups: *rigid arm* and *constant tension*. The constant-tension saws can be further divided into *C-arm* and *parallel-arm* saws.

Rigid-arm Saws

Rigid-arm saws (Illus. 7) have cast or tubular overarms that are stationary. The only visible movement is the blade going up and down. A spring-loaded plunger is located on the upper arm. With rigid-arm saws, the downstroke is the power stroke; the upstroke is produced by the spring action, located in the upper tube of the plunger assembly. In operation, the spring is loaded (or stretched out) on the downstroke (cutting stroke).

The drive system of the rigid-arm machine, by virtue of its design, is subjected to sudden loading and unloading of the blade tension during each stroke. In other words, the tension is not consistently the same throughout the entire stroke. If, because of feeding pressure or sawdust clogging, the upper spring does not pull the blade up, after the downstroke, the blade is too flexible as it is pushed upward by the drive system of the machine. This situation, combined with feed-

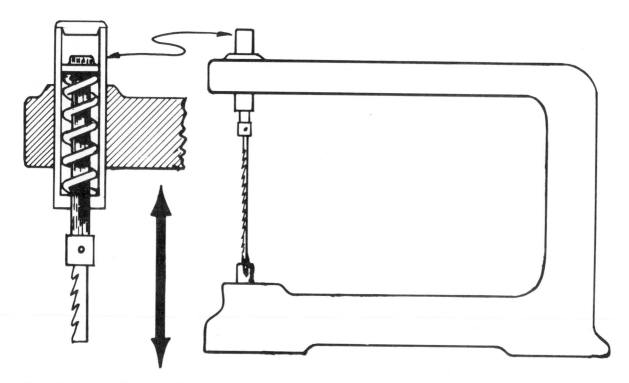

Illus. 7. How rigid-arm scroll saws work.

ing pressure, places strain on the blade; the result is premature breakage. To prevent this from happening, reduce stock thickness or use stiffer and wider blades; these blades, however, will progressively limit the sharpness of the turn that can be made and the capability of making intricate cuts in thicker material.

In short, the disadvantages of rigid-arm saws well outweigh their advantages. I would seriously question why one would purchase this type of machine for home or professional use.

Constant-Tension Saws

Constant-tension saws include the C-frame and parallel-arm types. (See Illus. 8 and 9.) Throughout the stroke, the blade always maintains exactly the same tension on the upstroke as it does on the downstroke. The advantages of constant-tension saws in-clude minimal blade breakage and the capability to cut with much thinner and narrower blades. This allows the operator to make incredibly sharp turns and saw accurate, highly detailed, intricate designs in thick as well as thin stock. As the blade reciprocates it enters slightly into the work on the downstroke and then backs away slightly on the upwards movement. (See Illus. 8 and 9 .) The cutting action of constant-tension saws is much different from that of the rigid-arm saws. On a rigid-arm saw, the saw blade stays perfectly vertical in just one spot, moving up and down only within its own space. With constant-tension saws, the blade generally moves slightly forward into the wood on the downwards stroke and slightly back on the upstroke, or vice versa. The blade can also have a "mixed action" movement.

The blade motion of constant-tension saws does several important things: (1) It generally provides for better sawdust removal when

10

fine blades are used, which means cooler cutting, less friction, and no burning of the cut; since less heat is generated, blades will stay sharp longer and don't break as often. (2) Some of the blade works against the walls or sides of the saw kerf; the results are extremely smoothly cut surfaces that need no or very little sanding. The blade "rasps" away ridges on the previously cut surfaces as it moves into and out of new wood during the reciprocating movement. (3) Less pressure is required to hold down the workpiece if the blade backs off on the upstroke, which is when the work normally tends to lift on the rigid-arm saws.

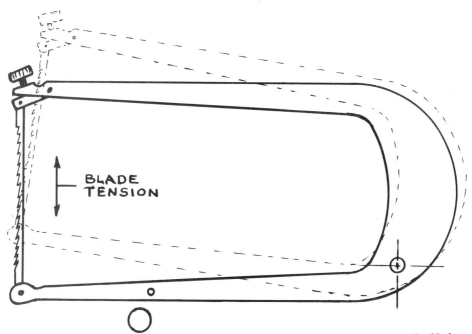

Illus. 8. The motion of a typical C-frame constant-tension scroll saw. Note the blade positions.

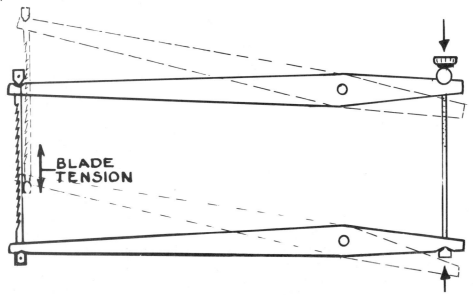

Illus. 9. The action of a true parallelogram constant-tension saw. Note the blade positions.

C-Arm Constant-Tension Saws. These saws are tensioned "up front." (See Illus. 8.) This is an advantage because it eliminates the reach to the back of the machine, where almost all parallel-arm saws are tensioned. (See Illus. 9.) The primary disadvantage of the C-arm saw design is the way the blade travels. As you can see in Illus. 8, the blade tips backwards on the upstroke. On some C-arm saws, the pivot point is even more centrally located, vertically; this means that when cutting, the blade tips slightly more forward than vertical, at the completion of the downstroke. The tipping of the blade in and out of a vertical plane creates some problems when sawing along sharp irregular curves in thicker stock. It's likely that the curved cuts will not be as square, as sharp, and as true as when making straight line cuts in the same material with the same saw.

Parallel-Arm Constant-Tension Saws. These saws (Illus. 9) are regarded by most authorities as the best overall—at least in design theory, and that is with all other considerations being equal. A cheaply made parallel-arm saw, for example, is no better a buy than a cheap version of any other tool. The major advantage of true parallelogram saws is that the blade remains vertical throughout the total stroke. Although the blade moves slightly into the cut on the downward stroke and moves slightly back on the upstroke, this design seems to produce the smoothest and truest cuts with the least blade breakage. In any case, a constant feed is most important for smooth cuts and blade life.

SCROLL SAW FEATURES

Blade suspension is one feature you will read about frequently in the chapters ahead. The term pertains to the way the blade is mounted to the forward ends of the C-arm or the parallel arms. It cannot be a "stiff" connection. The blade must hinge or pivot freely, even on the C-arm-type saws. Feeding pressure will cause the blade to bend, which is normal in fast cutting. When the feed is slowed to make a turn, the blade "catches up" and the cut made along the curve edge is vertical, as it should be.

There is a greater emphasis on the blade clamp's ability to pivot on parallel-arm-type saws than there is on the C-frame designs. Illus. 9 shows how the angle of the blade to the arm becomes more acute as the saw approaches the highest upward position of its stroke. Therefore, it is imperative that the blade is allowed to pivot freely. (See Illus. 10.) If the blade suspension system does not provide a good, free pivot action, the blade will be forced to bend at the point where it comes out of clamps. (See Illus. 11.) This causes strain and metal fatigue at this point; premature blade breakage is the certain result.

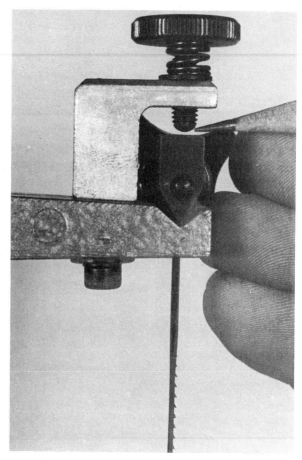

Illus. 10. A blade clamp pivots on a knife-like edge. The space above the clamp is intentional—it allows the blade clamp to pivot freely.

The bending of blades, shown in Illus. 11, can also be caused by careless installation. If the blade is not pointing in the right direction as it is clamped in the first blade holder or chuck, the blade must be bent to get the other end clamped. That's why some saws have locking pins. (See Illus. 12.) These pins hold the blade clamp steady while it is installed and tightened with a wrench.

Illus. 11. Saw blades bent near the ends indicate a poorly designed blade suspension system or careless blade installation. Bending, as shown, results in premature and more frequent blade breakage.

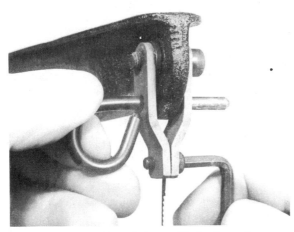

Illus. 12. A pivotal gimbal-type blade clamp has parallel jaws and a "locking pin" that's used to keep the clamp from "swinging around" when the blade is installed.

There are a lot of different types of saw tables available on the market today. When buying, pay attention to the following features: their shapes (round, rectangular, etc.), sizes, center openings, blade slots (for ease of blade installation), and their abilities to tilt right, left, or in either direction. Other important considerations include the accuracy of the tilting scale, the smoothness or ease of adjustment, and the clamp quality.

I sometimes find a large table a disadvantage because, since I seldom use the back of it, I just store unneeded pieces on it, which get in the way when I do need to swing a big piece of stock.

Pay attention to the design engineering (or lack of design engineering) on many of the new constant-tension saw tables. Some manufacturers advertise full 45° tilts either left or right, but some of these tables will not tilt to 45°. Others that do tilt to 45° do not permit cutting! On one machine, the lower arm strikes the saw table on the upstroke when it is set at just 34°, so you can't cut at 45° at all. On another machine, if you tilt the table a full 45° left (the only way the table tilts), you have less than ¼-inch clearance under the hold-down arm. On yet another machine, the hold-down arm must be removed to permit tilting the table to 45°.

One machine has a slot in the table that is either in the wrong location for a tilting operation or is just not big enough, because with the table tilted the blade cuts up the table and makes a very jagged blade opening. On another machine that must be bolted to the manufacturer's stand, the saw table strikes the stand just as it reaches the 45° tilt. In this case, your workpiece cannot be larger than the saw table, because if it extends over the edge of the table, the workpiece will strike the saw stand.

All these problems associated with poor table-tilt design can leave the potential customer shocked over the sloppy engineering that's evident in some machines and fairly well hidden by other manufacturers. For example, though full 45° cuts are not made that often on a scroll saw, the table should be designed to make that cut if that is what the manufacturer claims it can do. Why have a 45° mark on the scale if you can't even adjust the table to that setting?

A lot of design inefficiencies are the result of the manufacturer's intent to get a machine into the marketplace quickly without complete evaluation or testing. Several manufacturers make design changes and improvements as they go along. This is why it is essential for the buyer to be wary.

Make the following inspections when looking at a scroll saw: Check the side play of the arms. Look at the saw in operation to see if the travel of the saw blade is a blur or a crisp vertical line. Pay attention to saw vibration: Some saws are very loud and must be bolted down to a heavy workbench or special steel stand; otherwise, they bounce all over. Other saws run very quietly and so smoothly that you can actually balance a coin on its edge. (See Illus. 48.) The noise level can affect your health and comfort during extended periods of saw use.

Illus. 13. *This scroll saw has a smooth, vibration-free operation, as shown by the coin that is steadily balanced on edge while the scroll saw is on.*

One machine I am familiar with practically

requires a major overhaul just to change speeds. The guard must be removed, which is okay, but then the pulleys must be removed from the pitman shaft, reversed, aligned, and then secured again with two screws before the belt and guard are replaced. Another machine has one double pulley for speed changes, but no provision to adjust or move the motor.

A big throat capacity can be a disadvantage, especially if you have a saw with rear tensioning, because the adjustment control is difficult to reach on 19-, 24-, and 26-inch saws. On the other hand, if you cut a lot of large pieces, a big throat capacity is important. Also, remember that a tabletop machine that has a rear motor mount might require as much as three feet of space (front to back) for just a 19-inch throat capacity.

Check where the *switch* is; it should be easy to reach so the saw can be quickly shut down if necessary. An auxiliary foot switch is very useful for some kinds of sawing jobs, and it's a very good safety feature.

There are machines that require the use of a manufacturer's stand. Some stands take up considerably more floor space than is necessary. A stand should be solid, stand level, and not occupy excessive floor area.

Some machines have dust blowers. Some blowers work effectively; others either barely work at all or they can't be adjusted easily to the cutting area.

Foreign manufacturers are likely to require metric wrenches and metric replacement nuts and bolts. Believe it or not, one machine required one size allen wrench for the lower blade clamp, and a different size allen wrench to tighten the upper blade clamp. This is a problem the manufacturer should have corrected.

Weight and portability is an important feature for many woodcrafters. More weight does not necessarily mean a better value. Extra weight is one way for manufacturers to counteract machine vibration. If your saw must be stored away after every time it's used, or you use your saw at craft shows, portability is an essential consideration.

2

LIGHT-DUTY SCROLL SAW

Illus. 14 shows a bench top saw that can be used for light-duty sawing and—with the use of its accessory attachments—can perform many other light woodworking jobs.

The Sears saw is called the "Basic Scroll Saw/Sander"; with a flexible shaft and its accessories added it is a versatile hobby mini-shop. It has been around for many years. (The Scroll Saw/Sander is available at Sears, as are extra blades, sanding discs, and the 30-inch flexible shaft kit.) The overarm, table, and base are made of pressed sheet steel.

Illus. 14. The Sears Scroll Saw/Sander has a 15-inch throat capacity and can cut stock 1⅝ inches thick in soft wood.

The table measures 8 inches × 9½ inches and tilts 45° left and right. (See Illus. 16.) You can mount a 4-inch disc sander (Illus. 17 and 18) and a 30-inch flexible hose with a collet chuck to the side-mounted power takeoff drive. This is a "kitchen-table" workshop that's ideal for light craft work, making models, etc. It has suction cups on the base, and it does not have to be attached to a workbench unless desired. The saw alone has a total shipping weight of only 16 pounds, which makes it easy to carry around.

Its direct-drive motor provides enough power to handle most hobby projects. The saw blade is driven at a rate of 3,450 strokes per minute. Intricate cuts can be made in soft wood of up to 1⅝" thick and in harder woods up to ½" thick. Soft aluminum and brass can be cut up to a maximum of ¹⁄₁₆" thick.

. Using the accessory kits available, you can drill, sand, brush, deburr, carve, etc., using the power takeoff drive that drives a flexible shaft.

Whenever the power takeoff is used with an accessory the scroll-saw blade must be in position on the saw. The Sears saw carries a 3-inch pin-type blade. Illus. 19–21 show blade installation. A plastic blade guard is easy to remove or install without tools. It simply snaps into position with two pins that fit into matching holes on the arm. (See Illus. 22.)

This saw will cut softwoods up to 1¾ inch thick, but it is better suited to cutting thinner materials. The saw has a direct-drive motor that delivers 3,450 strokes per minute. The length of the stroke is not specified, but it is short. With continuous cutting of thin materials, the wear on the blade can be shifted by raising the table. This brings a new, unused segment of the blade to the cutting area.

The flexible shaft can be fitted with a drill; it can also be fitted with carving burrs, a sander, grinders, etc. (See Illus. 23.) The drill is used to make entry holes for threading the blade through the workpiece when making interior cuts. (See Illus. 24–26.) The Sears Hobby Saw has suction cups that firmly secure it to any smooth tabletop or bench top.

The Sears light-duty scroll saw is ideal for

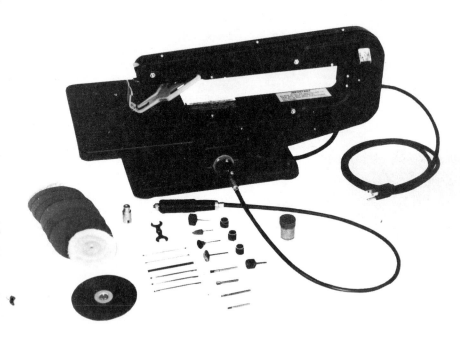

Illus. 15. The Sears saw with a flexible shaft and all accessories is a versatile hobby minishop.

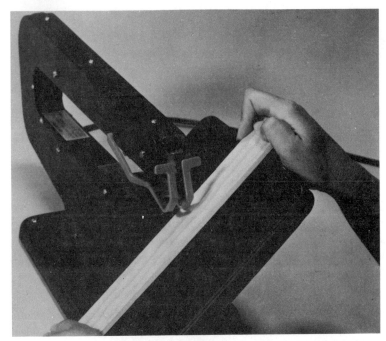

Illus. 16. Making a 45° cut with the Sears saw.

Illus. 17. Mounting the disc sander to the power takeoff.

Illus. 18. The disc sander smooths and shapes edges. Work must be held on the left or forward and downward side of the disc.

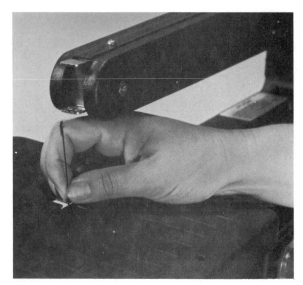

Illus. 19 (left). A close-up look at the upper blade holder. The pins set into the small "v's." The blade can be installed to cut in any of four directions.

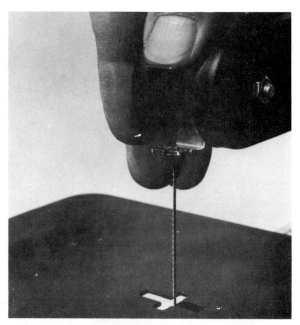

Illus. 20. The upper-blade lever holder is a spring that is depressed for blade installation. No tools are needed to change blades.

Illus. 21. A close-up look at the upper blade holder. The pins set into the small "v's." The blade can be installed to cut in any of four directions.

Illus. 22. The plastic blade guard. It does not function as a hold-down.

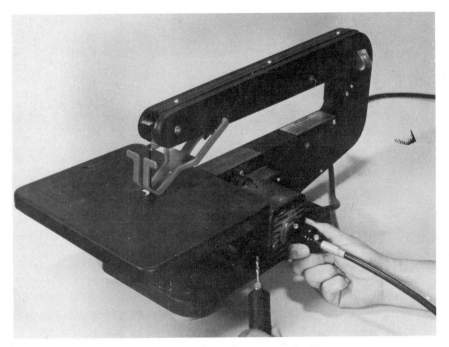

Illus 23. Attaching the flexible shaft to the power takeoff.

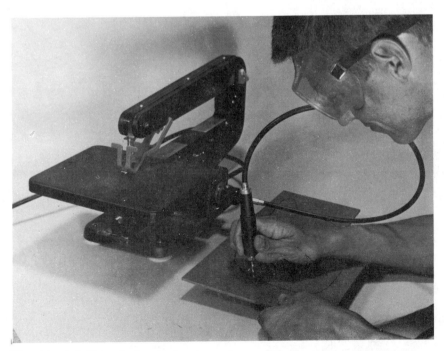

Illus 24. A drill in the hand piece is used to make an entry hole for the blade so that an inside cut can be made.

Illus. 25. Threading the blade through the drilled hole and reinstalling it.

Illus. 26. Making the inside cut.

cutting desk signs or letters and numbers for various uses. Illus. 27 shows the letter P being cut out from ¾" wood using a coarse blade in the scroller.

Patterns for letters and numbers are available at Sears through retail sales and its catalog. The Model 25196 Wood Sign Layout Kit has three styles of letters that come in three sizes, 2, 3, and 4".

Instructions are given for a simple sign layout system. There is no need to measure between letters because of the design of the stencils. A protective cover provided enables you to use the stencils over and over. The types of wood to use and finishing methods are explained in the instructions.

Illus. 27. Use the Wood Sign Layout Kit to transfer the letters to the wood. Saw to the carbon line using the scroll saw.

Illus. 28. Script style for a desk sign. The letters are cut through, leaving a thin strip at the bottom that holds the letters together and provides a way to attach the sign to the base.

Illus. 29. In this example, the letters have been cut out and attached to another board for a special effect. The style is Old English.

Illus. 30. In this case, the letters have been cut through and covered with black from behind. They can also be illuminated.

Illus. 31. Three styles of letter and number stencils from Sears Model 25196 Wood Sign Layout Kit are, as follow, from top to bottom: Old English, Script, and Block styles.

3

SEARS "WALKING BEAM" SCROLL SAW

The Sears "Walking Beam" scroll saw (Illus. 32 and 33) has some design elements that separate it from all other machines. However, the Walking Beam saw is still essentially a parallel-arm, constant-tension machine like many other saws available today.

The general specifications include an 18-inch throat, a 2-inch-maximum-thickness cutting capacity, a ⅞-inch stroke length with 1,700 cutting strokes per minute, and a direct-drive, rear-mounted motor with linkage to the lower arm. The machine will accept 5- to 6-inch plain-end blades and 5-inch pin-type blades. The worktable measures 9 inches × 14⅜ inches, and it has grooves for a mitre gauge attachment. The table also features two blade-holder "pockets" cast into the surface to ensure that the blade clamps are always attached with precisely the correct spacing from each other. (See Illus. 34.) The machine weight without the stand is only 26 pounds.

Illus. 32. The Sears 18-inch Walking Beam scroll saw on a four-leg stand.

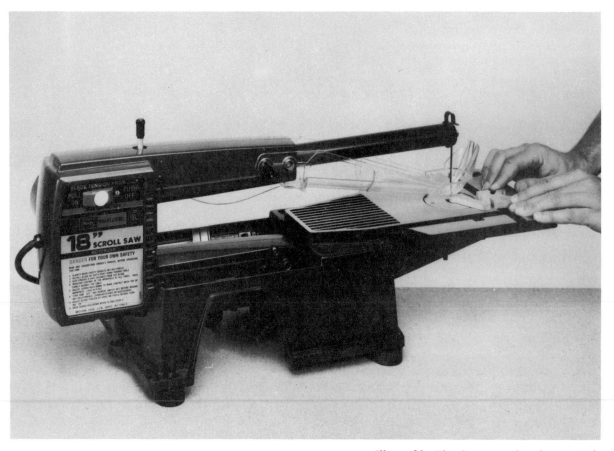

Illus. 33. The Sears saw bench-mounted.

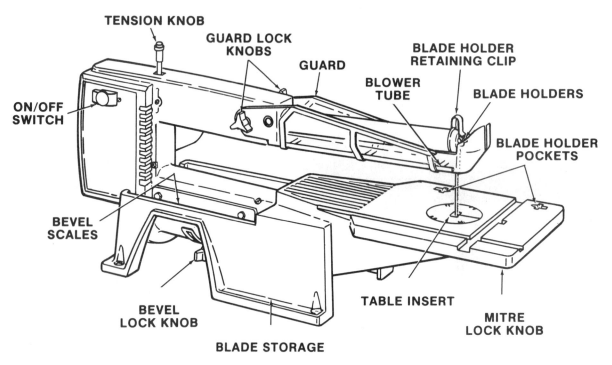

TENSION KNOB

GUARD LOCK KNOBS

GUARD

BLADE HOLDER RETAINING CLIP

BLOWER TUBE

BLADE HOLDERS

ON/OFF SWITCH

BLADE HOLDER POCKETS

BEVEL SCALES

BEVEL LOCK KNOB

BLADE STORAGE

TABLE INSERT

MITRE LOCK KNOB

Illus. 34. The basic features and controls of the Sears Walking Beam scroll saw.

The fan-cooled induction motor is mounted not below but in the rear housing, between the upper and lower arms. Illus. 35 and 36 show the housing and arms removed from the integral die-cast table and base. (See Illus. 37.) The table does not tilt. The entire motor-housing unit, with the arms, tilts in a sliding-bracket trunnion that fits into the base casting. Illus. 38 depicts bevel-sawing with the blade tilted instead of the table or workpiece being tilted. Illus. 34 and 39 show the tilt-control knob located under the base. Tilting of up to 45° in either direction is possible. The two arms consist of tubular construction with bearing pivot points at the ends of the main housing. (See Illus. 40.)

A plastic key locks the on-and-off switch. The key must be inserted correctly in order to activate the switch. This is an important safety feature that prevents unauthorized use of the machine. (See Illus. 41.)

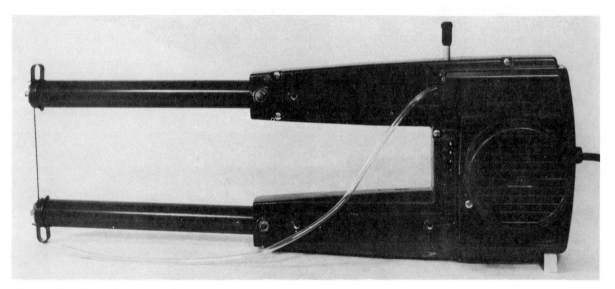

Illus. 35. The right side of the machine without the base, table, or guard; shown are the housing, motor cover, and air tubing.

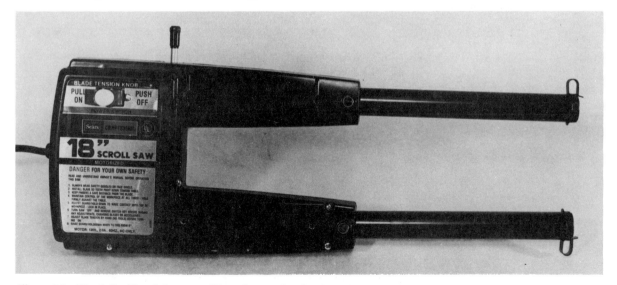

Illus. 36. The left side of the saw. Note the tension knob at the top and the motor switch.

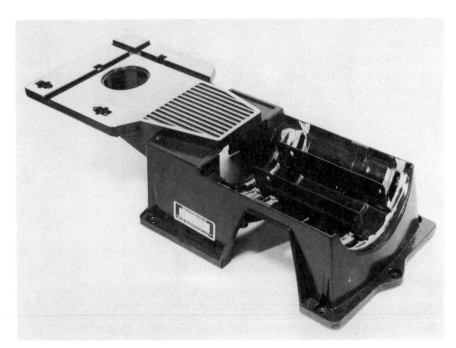

Illus. 37. Die-cast aluminum forms the integral base and non-tilting table.

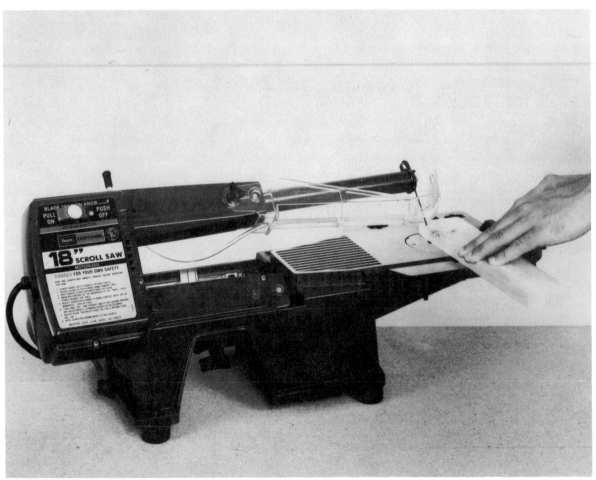

Illus. 38. The table surface and workpiece remain horizontal during bevel sawing. Instead, the blade is tilted.

Illus. 39. The tilt control knob is located under the base.

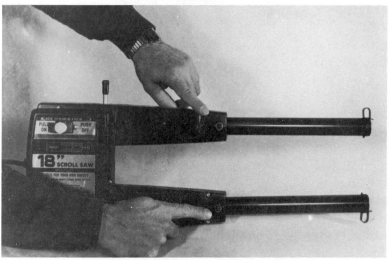

Illus. 40. Arm pivot points.

Illus. 41. To operate the machine, a plastic key has to be inserted.

The blade suspension system is based upon the action of the blade clamps that pivot on the ends of the hollow tubular arms. (See Illus. 42.) The versatile blade holders are designed to carry either plain-end blades or pin-type blades. (See Illus. 43.) As stated earlier, the blade holder pockets in the table verify correct blade length and positioning. A setscrew tightens plain-end blades. (See Illus. 44.) The blade holders are also of the four-position type, which means the blade can be installed with any one of the 90° orientation positions desired. "V's" cast into the blade holders actually permit pivoting on the "edges" of the slots in the end caps of the upper and lower arms. (See Illus. 46 and 47.) The retaining clips (see Illus. 34 and 47) do not touch the blade holders. Their purpose, supposedly, is to keep the blade holders in place if or when the blade breaks. Tension is provided by the tensioning knob with a clockwise turning direction. (See Illus. 48.) This saw has one serious limitation: The operator cannot make convenient and fast blade changes.

The operator's manual recommends the use of pin-end blades for cutting inside openings and piercing work. In order to allow for the pin of the blade, it is necessary to "drill an oversized hole in a scrap section of the workpiece." Pin-type blades do not come in the very fine sizes. Consequently, the ability to saw fine detail and make "on-the-spot" turns when doing interior or inside cutting is seriously limited. Plain-end blades can be used, but it is more difficult to fasten the blade holders to the blades.

Straight line cuts can sometimes be performed successfully using wide blades and slow feeds with the accessory mitre gauge. (See Illus. 49–51.) Sometimes the "burr" that exists on scroll saw blades during manufacturing interferes with a true straight-line cutting direction that's parallel to the blade direction. The Sears Walking Beam saw is best used for cutting curves in thinner materials. (See Illus. 52.)

The Sears Walking Beam saw must be bolted to the workbench or table if the metal stand is not used. Use rubber vibration-absorbing bumpers between the saw base and workbench.

The Sears Walking Beam scroll saw is ideal for cutting signs, intricate pattern cutting, etc. A variety of blades is available for cutting wood, plastic, metal, and other materials. Coarse blades for heavy cutting and thin blades for intricate cutting are stocked at Sears.

Illus. 42. The blade suspension of a Sears Walking Beam saw.

28

Illus. 43. Blade holders (above) will carry plain-end blades (left) or pin-type blades, as shown at the right.

Illus. 44. Here a blade is being clamped in the blade holders, which have been properly located by the "pockets" in the table.

Illus. 45. The lower blade holder is attached. Note the teeth pointing downwards.

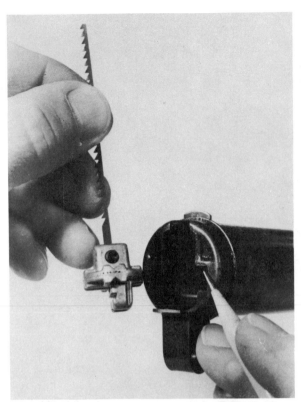

Illus. 46. The lower arm end. Note the slot in the end cap and "edges," which correspond to the "v's" of the blade holder and permit a pivoting action during the operation of the saw.

Illus. 47. The upper blade holder (clamp) in pivoting position on the edges of the arm's end cap. Note the inverted U-shape spring-retaining clip above the arm.

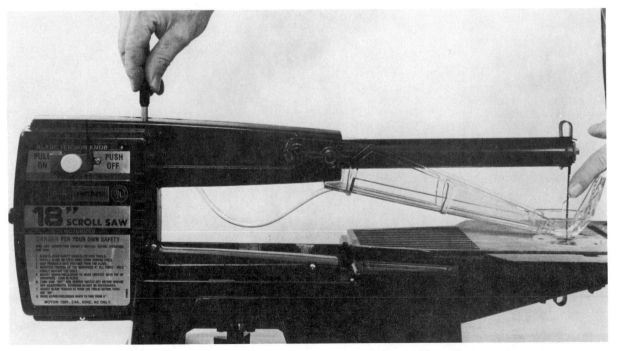

Illus. 48. Blade tensioning.

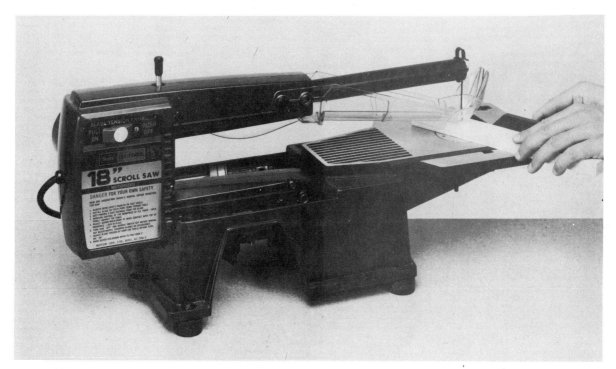

Illus. 49. Making a mitre cut.

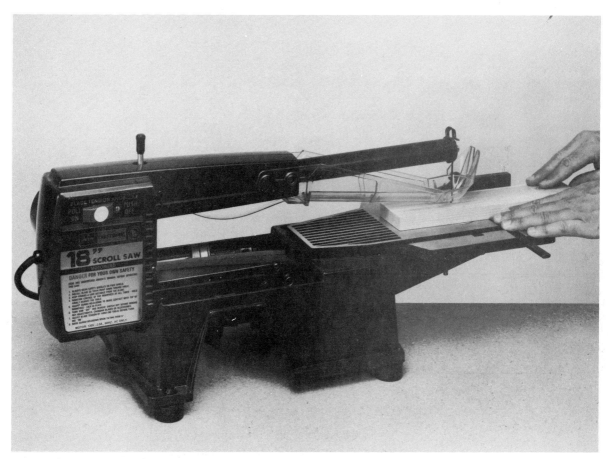

Illus. 50. Ripping, using the mitre gauge clamped to the table as a fence.

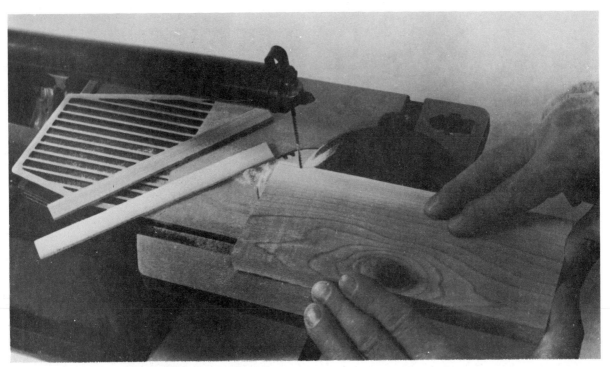

Illus. 51. Another view of the ripping procedure, with the guard removed for an easier operation.

Illus. 52. Making outside, curved cuts in thin material produces a smoothly cut surface. Thick materials cut proportionally slower. Note the use of the plastic hold-down guard.

This book contains many patterns that can be used with the scroll saw. Children's coloring books are another source for patterns. As mentioned in the previous chapter, sign layout kits are available for letter and number stencils. Sears has two such kits. The model number 25196 kit has patterns 2, 3″ and 4″ high. The model 25176 kit has stencils 6–8″ and 10″ high.

4

BLADES, SPEEDS, AND FEEDS

When the right *blade* (Illus. 53) is used on the material being cut, at the correct saw *speed* (cutting strokes per minute), and the operator feeds the material into the saw at the proper *rate*, the results will be an efficient cutting operation. (See Illus. 54.) That is, the wood (or material) will be cut with the smoothest finish, in the quickest time; also, there will be the least amount of wear and tear possible on the machine and minimal blade breakage if the blades were installed properly and used at the correct tension. With each new scroll-sawing experience, it becomes easier to coordinate these three basic factors. (If your machine is of a single-speed type, then you only have to concentrate on the blade selection and feed rate.)

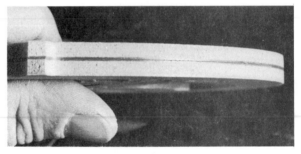

Illus. 54. Two thicknesses of ¼-inch hardwood plywood. The cut surface is so smooth it shines, and there is no splintering on the lower edge.

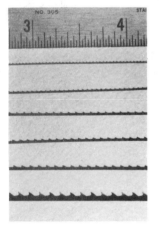

Illus. 53. Common fret-saw blades used in constant-tension saws. Above, a 2/0 fine blade with 28 teeth per inch. Below, a coarse blade with 9 teeth per inch.

TYPES OF BLADES

Scroll saw blades are reasonably inexpensive, at least when compared to other cutting tools and to the price of a piece of good sandpaper.

Traditionally, saw blades used in reciprocating sawing machines are of four basic types. These are: the plain-end blade (Illus. 55), the pin-type blade (Illus. 56), the sabre saw blade (Illus. 57), which is the widest and stiffest, and spiral blades (Illus. 58 and 59).

Today, however, the most widely used blades are the 5-inch plain-end blades, because this type of blade is used in almost all scroll saws. The narrower-sized blades are emphasized because with them the popular constant-tension saws will cut very sharp turns in thick and thin stock. In recent years, more attention has been given to the finer fret saw blades because they have proven reliable when used in the constant-tension saws.

Illus. 56. Three-inch pin-end blades used in Sears hobby scroll saws.

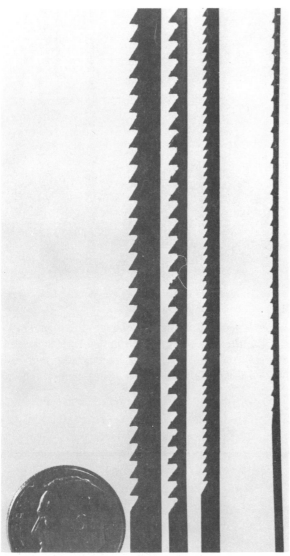

Illus. 55. Standard 5-inch, plain-end blades; the dime is for size comparison. From left to right: 10-tooth Delta scroll-saw blade, 10-tooth Trojan scroll-saw blade, 20-tooth Olson scroll-saw blade, and a No. 7 skip-tooth fret blade with 14 teeth per inch.

Illus. 57. Sabre-saw blades have 9 teeth per inch, are 3/16 or 1/4 inch in width, and chucked at one end, as shown. These blades are only used on rigid-arm scroll saws.

Illus. 58. These five-inch spiral blades, supplied by the Olson Saw Co., cut in all directions. They range from a 2/0 size (.025-inch kerf) at the right up to a No. 6 (.049) at the left. These are toothed blades that are twisted.

Illus. 59. At left: the Olson No. 6 spiral blade with 30 teeth per inch. At right: a length of Remington's rod saw that has particles of tungsten carbide bonded to a steel rod. This rod saw is recommended only for very hard materials like marble, glass, and ceramics.

Illus. 60. Teeth sizes are specified as the number per inch. Here we have a skip-tooth configuration fret blade with 20 teeth per inch.

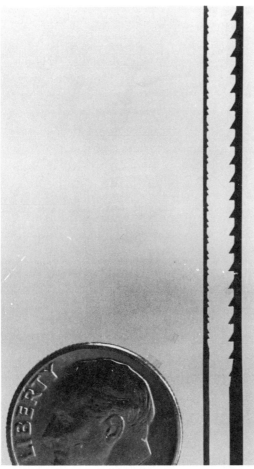

Illus. 61. Fret-saw blades by Eberle, (a German manufacturer). On the left, a 2/0 blade. On the right, a No. 9 blade.

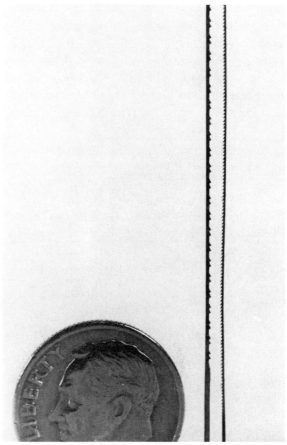

Illus. 62. The No. 5 skip-tooth fret blade on the left is being compared to a No. 5 jewellers' metal-cutting blade on the right. Respectively, they have 14 and 36 teeth per inch.

Jewellers' or metal-piercing blades have regular saw teeth. They are made of hardened, tempered steel for cutting mild steel and other hard materials. They range in size from 8/0 to No. 12. Only those sizes from a No. 1 (.012 inch thick, .024 inch wide) up to the No. 12 (.023 inch thick, .070 inch wide) are recommended for motor-driven scroll saws. Jewellers' blades are not recommended for normal wood-cutting jobs, although some saw users do attempt to cut veneer with fine jewellers' blades. Silas Kopf, a marquetry expert, says "Jeweller's blades have the teeth too close together, and they can clog." Kopf recommends skip double-tooth blades for cutting wood veneer because they clear the dust away. Illus. 62 compares a 5/0 jewellers' blade to a 5/0 fret blade.

Spiral blades are unique because they saw in all directions without turning the workpiece. They are ideal for cutting small curves and openings in detailed fretwork, for 0° radius work, etc. Some 30 to 40 years ago, a wirelike blade with helical teeth was used in light crafts. At that time the blades were called drill saws. These blades also cut in any direction, but the shallow teeth limited their usefulness to just thin, soft materials. The spiral blades shown in Illus. 58 are a recent development by the Olson Saw Company. These are actually high-carbon steel, 5-inch blades with standard tooth forms that are twisted. They cut all kinds and thicknesses of material.

In addition to wood, spiral blades will cut nonferrous metals, plaster, bone, etc. Olson manufactures blades in 8 different sizes, from the smallest 2/0 with 51 teeth per inch, up to a No. 6 with 30 teeth per inch. The No. 6 cuts a big .049-inch kerf, which you might not want. It also kicks up a lot of sawdust. However, for some jobs, the No. 6 saw blade may be just what one needs.

Though the taut, highly tensioned fret saw blades permit on-the-spot turns, which might be considered a zero-radius turning capability, spiral blades can cut in all directions. However, although I have used spiral blades, I would not consider them a substitute or a cure-all for the standard fret blades. It is much easier to follow lines of larger radius curves and make straight line cuts with a fret blade than with a spiral blade. The spiral blade goes in all directions, often following the grain of the wood rather than the layout line. This makes it difficult to cut smooth, flowing curves without bumps or dips. Also, they do not cut surfaces nearly as smoothly as regular fret blades.

I did find one class of work for spiral blades that no other blade can handle—bevel-sawing letters for signs that all have to slant in the same direction. (See Illus. 63.) Illus. 64 shows the actual bevel-cutting with a spiral blade.

Illus. 63. A spiral blade is the only type of blade that can be used on a bevel-cut project such as this.

Illus. 64. When bevel-cutting with a spiral blade, you can cut in all directions without turning the workpiece.

Guidelines for Selecting Blades

It is difficult to make very specific recommendations in blade selection because of the following reasons: (1) The industry is not completely standardized. A number of variations among manufacturers do exist when scroll saw blades made by foreign manufacturers are included. (2) The performance of blades can vary from "batch to batch." For example, you may be able to put one blade to a lot of tension and get extensive use from it; however, though the next blade is identical to the first one, the second one will dull or snap in less than half the time, even though all of the other conditions appear the same. (3) The human element plays a part in determining which blade to use, because individual judgments are different. What is considered a moderate feed rate to one person can be interpreted as something entirely different by another individual.

There is no one blade that is the absolute best for a given job. Each blade will handle a range of jobs with various materials and different thicknesses. However, keep in mind these general guidelines for blade selection: The finer the blade, the less the thickness that can be cut without problems. With thick stock and thin blades, the feed must be slower; the results will be a smoother cut and less frequent blade breakage.

The first time I got my hands on a new constant-tension saw, I installed the finest blade on hand (a 2/0) and tried to cut ¾-inch hardwood—an unrealistic expectation. Remember, the thinnest blades are for the thinner materials. However, also remember that medium-size fret blades such as those in the 5 to 9 range are still very narrow when compared to the blades widely used for conventional cutting jobs with rigid-arm scroll saws.

One more general guideline should be noted: As the thickness of material increases, use blades with proportional fewer teeth. In short, use a coarse blade for thick material. Illus. 65 illustrates the importance of having at least two, preferably three, teeth in contact with the workpiece. Because of the unique capabilities of the constant-tension saws, blades that are finer than usual can sometimes be used to cut thicker materials. However, don't feed the material too quickly. More tension is required; slow the feed rate at curves to avoid bellied or unsquare cuts. (See Illus. 66.) The amount of detail of your particular project is very specifically related to blade selection. Always use the widest blade possible, but one that will still allow you to make the desired curves with ease.

The chart on page 40 is based on blades available at Sears. It should provide guidelines for selecting the proper blade to use for a particular range of cutting jobs. The blade you choose should be based upon the following factors: operating and cutting speeds, quality of cut, and blade durability (wear and breakage) desired.

Illus. 65. At least two, preferably three, teeth should be in contact with the material at all times. Here, for example, a Sears 15-teeth-per-inch blade is a good choice for sawing this ¼" material.

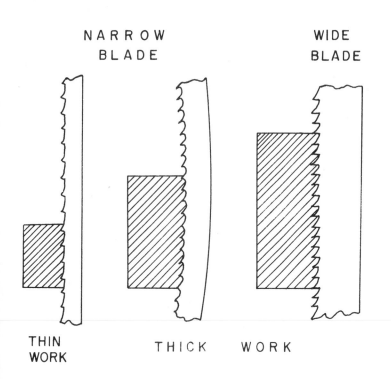

NARROW BLADE

WIDE BLADE

THIN WORK

THICK WORK

Illus. 66. The effect of blade width, feeding pressure, and material thickness.

Table 1
Scroll Saw Blades Available at Sears for Use with the
Walking Beam (18") Scroller and the 16" Scroll Saw

Feature	Material To Be Cut	Description	Length	TPI	Width	Thickness
Extra-Thin Cuts	Marquetry, Softwood	Pin-Type	5″	18	.055	.010
Extra-Thin Cuts	Soft Wood	Pin-Type	5″	25	.065	.010
Fine Cuts	Thin Steel, Brass, Copper, Aluminum and Wood up to 1″	Pin-Type	5″	20	.110	.020
Fine Cuts, Medium Turns	Wood up to 1½″, Bone, Ivory, Aluminum, Pressed Wood	Pin-Type	5″	15	.110	.020
Straight, Fast Cuts and Medium Turns	Wood up to 1¾″, Bone, Ivory, Aluminum, Pressed Wood	Pin-Type	5″	10	.110	.020
Extremely Thin, Narrow Cuts	Hard Rubber, Bakelite, Wood, Ivory, Thin Plastic	Blank-End	5″	20	.035	.020
Heavy Duty, for Fast Cutting	All Woods up to Saw's Capacity	Blank-End	5″	7	.250	.020
Fast, Straight Cuts or Wide Turns	.062 to .125″ Thick Steel, Copper, Brass, Aluminum	Blank-End	6″	20	.250	.028

The jigsaw or scroll saw is the safest of all power tools. It is versatile and can cut wood, metal, steel, iron, lead, plastics, paper, cloth, pressboard, and many other materials. It is used for a wide variety of jobs, including the making of jigsaw puzzles the old-fashioned way.

A wide assortment of blades is available and sold by Sears for every cutting need. In general, the basic blade types available are as follows: thin, fine-tooth blades for sawing thin woods and metals, veneers, plastics, and similar materials; medium-tooth blades for sawing wood and metals of medium thickness; and coarse-tooth blades for heavier sawing in thicker materials.

A jigsaw or scroll saw operates effectively only when equipped with the right blade for the material to be sawed. For example, a wide blade cannot make sharp turns, and a coarse blade is impractical for sawing thin stock. To help you choose the right blade for the job on hand, the proper Sears blades for every operation are listed.

WOOD SAWING

For sawing soft woods ¾" thick or thicker, we recommend a blade with 7–10 teeth per inch. For hard woods, use a blade with 10–20 teeth per inch, depending on the type of turns required. For hard wood ¾" thick or thicker, use a blade with 10–15 teeth per inch.

In general, the thinner the material to be cut, the more teeth per inch there should be in the Sears blade used. The coarser the teeth in the blade, the faster the cutting will be. However, where sanding is to be kept to a minimum, it is often more practical to use a finer-tooth blade to minimize the surface tearing of the edges cut.

METAL SAWING

Cutting metal is much like cutting wood except that slower speeds are recommended and finer-tooth blades should be used. Aluminum can be cut at fairly high speeds and with coarse teeth, but harder metals require finer teeth and slower speeds. When sawing metals, always lubricate the blade with beeswax or paraffin. This will greatly prolong the life of the blade and result in much more efficient sawing.

Soft nonferrous metals such as brass, aluminum, pewter, and copper of a thickness of ⅛" or more definitely require a blade with 15 or more teeth per inch. For soft metals less than ⅛" in thickness, finer-tooth blades are recommended.

CUTTING THIN STOCK

When thin stock in wood is being cut, particularly veneer and thin plywood, the underedge of the material is frequently broken or chipped by the action of the blade. When thin metal is sawed, this same action often turns down the sawed edges. This can be overcome in two ways. The thin metal or other material can be sandwiched between two pieces of ⅛" wood. Thus, the outside of the wood will support the material and eliminate its breaking or bending while being sawed. A sheet of waxed paper included in this "sandwich" when sawing metals will automatically lubricate the blade.

TIPS ON BLADE USE

The 90° blade-twist trick (Illus. 67) is a technique that may be practical in some situations. To change the cutting direction of a blade, simply twist it on the ends. When it is twisted to 90°, you can feed the work from the side of the machine like a band saw. Most blades are not tempered at the ends so they can bend without breaking. Remember, however, that when the 90° blade-twist trick is done with C-arm and parallel-arm constant-tension saws, the result will be a less-than-ideal cutting stroke. In both cases, the arm action is such that the blade moves slightly from the back to the front of the machine with every stroke.

Most blade manufacturers package the blades in little bundles of a dozen wrapped with very fine wire. Getting a blade out of a bundle can at times be frustrating and time-consuming. If all the wire wrappings are removed, the blades can become mixed with other sizes; this makes it difficult for you to pick out the correct size. Lengths of ½-inch PVC (polyvinylchloride) plastic pipe with end caps or a cork make good storage ves-

sels. (See Illus. 68.) PVC components are available at most hardware stores and plumbing supply centers. One final tip: Attach a length of adhesive-backed magnetic tape to an appropriate spot on the saw base or stand. This will hold a selection of blades conveniently. (See Illus. 69.)

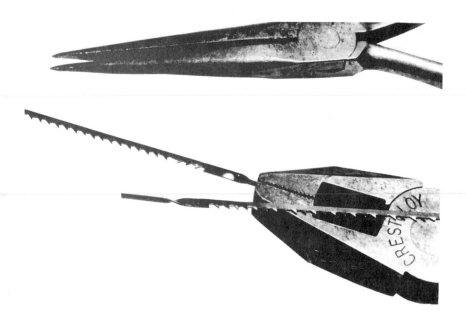

Illus. 67. When the ends of a blade are twisted, longer cuts can be made in a "band-saw fashion," which is feeding from the side, rather than the front of the machine.

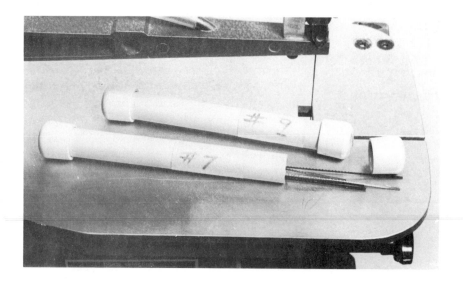

Illus. 68. One-half-inch-diameter PVC pipe and end caps make good blade storage containers.

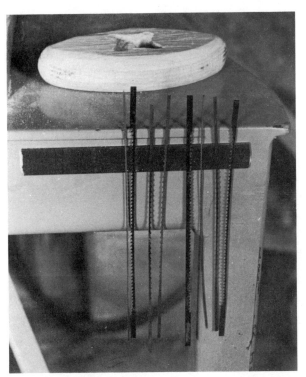

Illus. 69. A selection of blades can be kept conveniently ready with a length of adhesive-backed magnetic tape.

SPEEDS

Machine speed (strokes per minute) is not as important as the rate or speed at which the operator advances the material into the reciprocating new blade. Different feed rates mean different quality cuts. Commonsense regarding feed rates can prevent problems that might arise when using a single-speed machine. For almost all wood-sawing, the highest machine speed is best anyway—especially when the constant-tension saws are used. The only times slower speeds are important are when cutting unusually hard materials like hard metals and plastics. And slower speeds are normally best for sawing thin veneers, soft metals, bone, ivory, rubber, and laminated plastics.

Most one-speed or two-speed machines have around 1,200 to 1,800 cutting strokes per minute at the maximum. Hardwoods, softwoods, hardboard, plywood, and paper products over 1/16 inch thick can generally all be cut at the higher speeds. This covers about 95 percent of general wood-cutting

jobs. Medium machine speeds may be an advantage for cutting 1/16- to 1/4-inch-thick softwoods, for making puzzles and some inlay work. Cutting marquetry work and jewellery making are often best done at slower speeds, from less than 100 to 600 or 800 csm. Remember, for efficient cutting, as your material thickness increases, select wider blades with fewer teeth per inch.

FEEDS

If you occasionally cut materials such as soft metals or thin veneer-like wood and slow cutting speeds are recommended, you can often get by just by slowing the feed rate. As a general rule, slower feed rates result in a smoother finish on the cut surface. However, the best blade for the material being cut is one that not only produces smoothly cut surfaces but also is the most efficient as far as time is concerned.

Since feed rate is related to time and quality or smoothness of cut, let's look at a few examples. Illus. 70 shows a cut surface across the grain on 3/4-inch-thick white pine. A No. 9 fret blade with 11½ teeth per inch was used. The first inch at the left in the photo was cut at a rate of 10 seconds per inch of feed. The remainder of the cut was made at more than double that speed, cutting at the rate of 4 seconds per inch. Notice the obvious difference in surface quality. (Incidentally, pine is not one of the smoothest cutting woods. Walnut can burn at high cutting speeds, and poplar, a softwood, cuts smoothly and doesn't burn at high speeds.)

Illus. 71 shows three different finish qualities on hard maple. The first inch at the left in the photo was cut with a No. 9 fret blade with 11½ teeth per inch at a feed rate of 12 seconds per inch. The next inch was cut with the same blade but at three times the feed rate (4 seconds per inch). The final inch at the right was cut slowly, but on a band saw using a 1/4-inch skip-tooth blade.

Illus. 72 shows 3/4-inch red oak that was cut at two dramatically different rates. There was not a great deal of difference in the appearance of the surface qualities. However, tear-out on the bottom was greater at the faster feed rate. Slowing to a feed rate of about 6 or 7 seconds per inch increased surface quality considerably.

Illus. 70. Three-quarter-inch pine cut at different feed rates. The inch at left was cut in 10 seconds; the remainder of the cut was made at a rate of 4 seconds per inch of cut surface. Note the bottom tear-out.

Illus. 71. Differently cut surfaces of hard maple. The one at left was cut at a feed rate ⅓ the speed of the center cut. The cut on the right was made on a band saw.

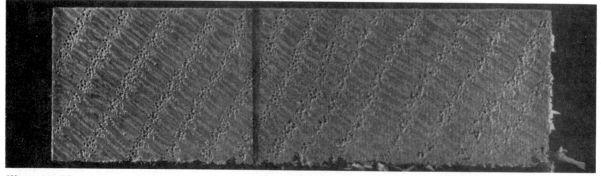

Illus. 72. Three-quarter-inch red oak: the cut at the left was made at 10 seconds per inch, and the rest of the cut was made at a feed rate of 4 seconds per inch.

SAWING TECHNIQUES

5

SAFETY

A scroll saw is probably the least hazardous power tool to use. However, this does not mean accidents cannot occur. A scroll saw is a machine tool, which means that everyone—beginners and professionals alike—should use it with respect and caution.

A scroll saw is ideal, however, for anyone starting woodcrafting. If beginners are using it, supervise them carefully. In addition to instructing them about the benefits gained

from scroll saw woodcrafting, teach them safety procedures and emphasize a respect for all tools and equipment. (See Illus. 73.)

Some adults may not take these safety procedures seriously, probably because manufacturers and sales personnel emphasize the comparatively safe and simple use of scroll saws. However, they too should pay careful attention to all safety guidelines.

There can be some potentially hazardous

Illus. 73. Note that the hands are well to each side of the blade. Always wear safety glasses. Do not wear jewelry.

situations when using a scroll saw. One is the unlikely probability that a blade might pierce your hand or fingers when it breaks. (See Illus. 74.) However, a good machine will have a mechanism to stop the motion of the upper arm the instant a blade breaks, which can only happen on a certain area of the blade. As an added precaution measure, however, make sure you do not put your fingers close to the blade action when using smaller blades. Normally, when larger blades are used, you are cutting larger and thicker work; therefore, your hands are, of necessity, farther from the blade. It might be a good idea to find out from the manufacturer or salesman what would happen to your machine if a blade breaks in an undesirable location and at an inopportune time.

A foot switch is a good option because you can immediately shut down the saw without having to first find the switch and move your hand to turn off the power. (See Illus. 75.) The foot switch is also an especially convenient and timesaving accessory. When thin stock is sawed or highly detailed cuts are being made, the saw blade may lift the material on the upstroke. A foot switch allows you to use both hands, with confidence, to help hold the work down against the table.

The scroll saw user will learn ways to pre-

Illus. 74. The way this broken blade damaged the project before the power could be stopped should be sufficient warning to keep your fingers at a safe distance from the blade. (Note: On some machines, the arm is designed to kick up and stop reciprocation immediately when the blade breaks.)

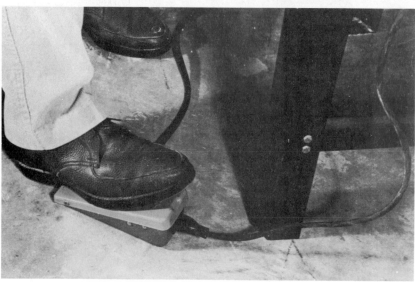

Illus. 75. A foot switch frees both hands for full control of the workpiece. If a blade snaps, you can shut down the saw immediately without removing your hands from the workpiece.

vent the workpiece from lifting and fluttering on the table as he gains experience. Hold-downs sometimes work, but are not always practical because of the size or nature of the workpiece. If the work is caught by the blade, the blade will lift the workpiece on the upstroke—it's at that time when your fingers can become pinched between the work and the table, or between the work and a hold-down that isn't adjusted properly. When constant-tension saws are used to make sharp turns, the workpiece is turned faster than when band saws or rigid-arm scroll saws are used. You have to learn how to make quick turns while applying pressure downwards on the workpiece, a skill that takes some practice to develop the right coordination. As you practice, the blade may catch in the workpiece and chatter up and down. With experience, you'll soon overcome this problem.

Another potentially dangerous situation exists when sawing thick stock. It's easy to become so mesmerized by the action of the blade that you forget where your hands and fingers are. If they are on top of the workpiece as they guide it around and under a moving overarm, they may get pinched. (See Illus. 76 and 77.)

Magnifying lights help some people follow the cutting line. (See Illus. 78.) They are also highly recommended for extremely detailed and precise cutting jobs. However, be careful when using a magnifying light on a constant-tension saw. Make sure it is adjusted properly; that is, that it is safely away from the up movement of the upper arm so it doesn't get banged when you turn the power on. Also, don't attempt to adjust a light and/or a magnifier with the power on. Magnification distorts the image under the glass and you might inadvertently move the light into a position where it can be hit by the oscillating arm. It is also important that the lamp be positioned so the safety spring device that lifts and stops the arm movement will not cause the arm to strike the lamp the instant a blade breaks. (See Illus. 79.)

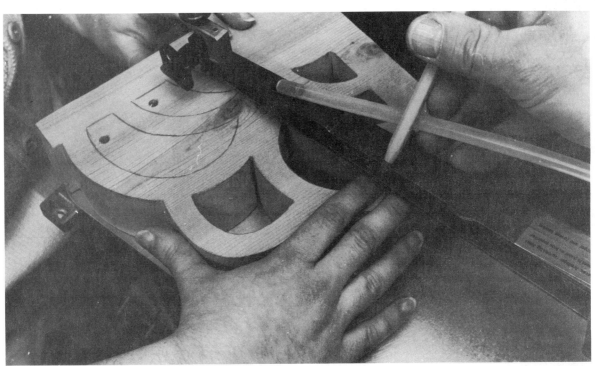

Illus. 76. Use caution when cutting thick stock so fingers do not become pinched between a moving saw arm and the workpiece.

Illus. 77. A similar situation with thick wood. Here, fingers are pinched under the thumbscrew of the blade clamp.

Illus. 78. A properly positioned magnifying light is a great accessory. However, distortion is such that it may take some practice to work out safe eye-to-hand coordination.

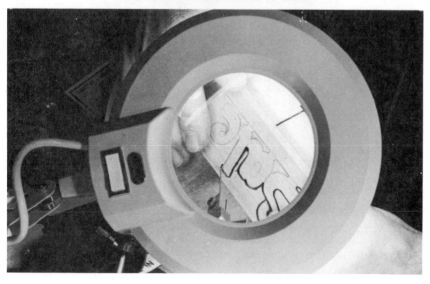

Illus. 79. Though things look bigger under magnification, they are also distorted; also, the normal hand reference points are somewhat different.

Here are some general safety rules that apply to scroll saws and power tools in general:

1. Know your machine; read and study the owner's manual carefully. You have to know the machine's capacities, limitations, and any special operational conditions that might be hazardous.

2. Caution: Most machines *should not* be lifted by the upper arm when they are being carried or moved. Lift by the base or stand.

3. Make sure the machine is properly grounded with a three-prong plug that is plugged into an appropriately grounded electric receptacle.

4. Always keep hands and fingers out of the line of cut; that is, away from the front of the blade.

5. Do not operate the scroll saw in dangerous environments, such as in damp or wet basements and workshops.

6. Dress appropriately; pull back long or loose hair and do not wear loose jewellery or clothing that could get tangled up in the moving parts of the saw.

7. Wear goggles or approved safety glasses. A dust mask is recommended during extensive use.

8. Make sure the workshop is child proof. Lock master switches, remove starter keys, and make sure that unauthorized individuals cannot obtain entry to or use of the machines.

9. Disconnect the power when servicing, installing accessories, lubricating and changing blades, etc. Avoid accidental start-ups; make sure the switch is off when plugging into the power supply.

10. Do not leave a machine unattended with the power on and running.

11. Use all appropriate guards.

12. Remove all adjusting keys, wrenches, blade chuck stiffeners, and similar devices before turning the power on.

13. Use extra precautions when cutting small pieces.

14. Do not operate tools while under the influence of drugs, alcohol, or medication.

15. Use approved accessories. If in doubt, consult with the manufacturer.

16. Keep floors and work areas clean so you don't trip on scraps, cords, or other items.

17. Do not rush by forcing the machine. If it isn't cutting as fast as you think it should, something needs correcting. Perhaps the blade being used is not the correct one or is dull; maybe something in the machine needs investigation.

18. Keep observers and visitors at a safe distance.

19. Do not exceed the specified capacities of the machine.

20. Slow down the feed rate before the work is suddenly freed at the completion of a cut.

21. Use sharp blades. Dull blades slow cutting efficiency and require extra feeding pressure.

22. Avoid cutting stock that does not sit flat on the worktable. Cutting dowels and similar objects requires special precautions and special work-holding fixtures.

23. Lubricate and maintain machines as recommended by the manufacturer.

24. Clean and remove accumulation of sawdust from moving parts. Remove deposits of pitch from the worktable immediately with a solvent, and then apply a coat of paste wax.

25. Slack off the blade tension at the end of each day or when the machine will not be used for a period of time.

26. Think and practice safety at all times.

6
SAWING BASICS

Elementary scroll-sawing techniques can be quickly mastered, but performing them accurately is essential to becoming a skilled scroll saw craftsperson. Following is a discussion of these basic but essential techniques.

PRE-CUT PREPARATIONS

Preparing the Machine

Getting the machine ready for use includes many of the obvious details, such as selecting the best blade, and installing and tensioning it. (See Illus. 80.) The owner's manual should provide all the necessary information about blade installation, tensioning, and other necessary operating adjustments and instructions.

Squaring the Saw Table

Square the saw table to the blade. All of the basic jobs discussed in this chapter will be done with the table adjusted precisely at 90° to the blade. One way to do this is to read the tilt scale and tighten the clamp at the zero setting. However, you can trust the scale markings on very few machines.

There are two other ways that are much better and more certain. Simply align the table to the blade with a good square, as shown in Illus. 81. Another, very quick method is done with a piece of thick scrap wood. Make a shallow cut, just deep enough to mark the wood, as shown in Illus. 82. Turn the stock end for end and bring it up behind the blade. If the blade lines up with the cut, the table is square. (See Illus. 83.) If it does not, adjust the table *slightly* (about half of what is off) and repeat the procedure.

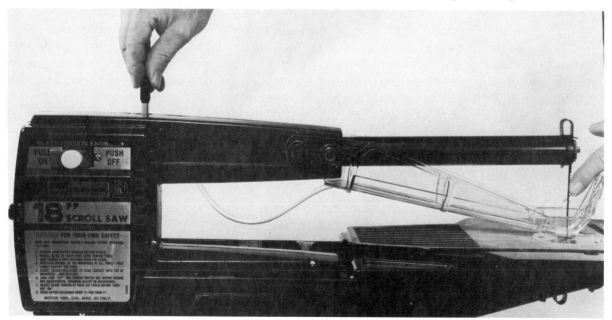

Illus. 80. When preparing the machine for sawing, make sure that the blade is retensioned before starting it.

Illus. 81. Using a square to check table adjustment.

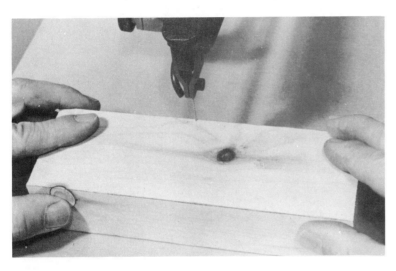

Illus. 82. A shallow cut is the first step in checking table squareness with thick scrap stock.

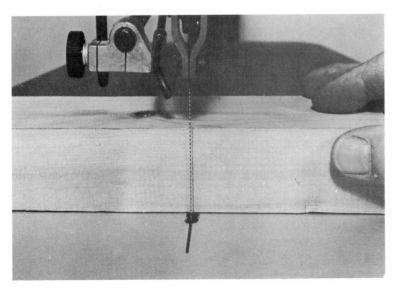

Illus. 83. Turn the stock around and bring it up behind the blade next to the shallow kerf. If the table is square, the back of the blade will slide easily into the kerf (cut).

CUTTING TECHNIQUES

Sitting Versus Standing

Is it better to sit or stand when cutting? Sitting is generally recommended, especially for long-term sawing. This requires a stool of an appropriate or adjustable height so that you do not have to hunch over your work. One of the problems in sitting is that you're not always well-balanced or mobile. Also, when sitting on a stool close to the saw, it is difficult to swing large pieces around without striking your body.

A sitting position makes using a foot pedal easier. When your weight is on a stool, your foot can comfortably actuate the foot switch. There is no need to reach for the scroll saw's switch while both your hands are guiding the workpiece. After using a foot switch several times, you will always want to use one.

Sears has a plug-in foot pedal control for just this purpose. It can be used on 110-volt tools that require up to 10 amperes. Illus. 84 shows this accessory. Note the non-skid base and 8' power cord.

Starting Points

The best starting point in cutting out any design is at a point or corner. Take a simple heart shape, for example; begin the cut so that you come into the pattern at the point of the heart. (See Illus. 85.) This is a much better starting point than beginning the cut on the side. (See Illus. 86.) When you come around and meet your starting point, it is difficult to make that part of the cut a flowing curve that intersects smoothly with the start. (See Illus. 87.)

When cutting out a circular shape like a disc or a toy wheel, it's best to come into the pattern layout line in a crosscutting (across the grain) direction. Also, it is far better to have a starting point on an outside curve, as in Illus. 87, than an inside curve. It's easier to sand away knobs or wavy lines that result from "coming around" and meeting up with the starting point.

Illus. 84. The Sears Model 25177 foot-actuated switch is designed for routers, drills, or scroll saws.

Illus. 85. Starting cuts at a point or corner is better than starting them on a curve.

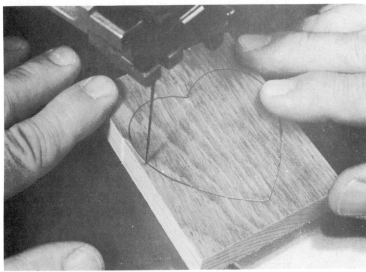

Illus. 86. This is not the best starting point for making this cutout. This is a "ripping" starting point that's cut with the grain.

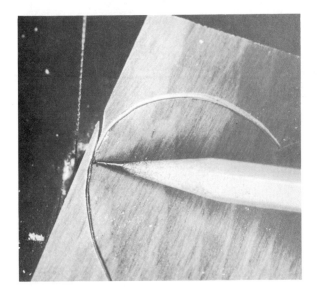

Illus. 87. Coming around to smoothly intersect with your starting point is more difficult when the cut is started in a direction that's with the grain, as shown.

Layout Line

Should you save the layout line (Illus. 88) or cut on it (Illus. 89)? The answer depends upon the type of project being made and the smoothness or quality of the saw cut. With most projects it will not make any difference.

Illus. 88. Following a layout line and "saving-the-line" by sawing on the waste side.

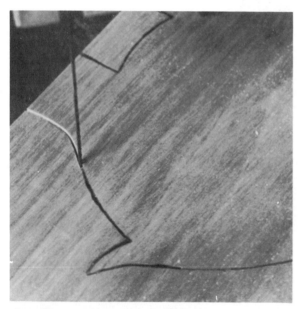

Illus. 89. Sawing right on the line.

If you are cutting with a conventional rigid-arm saw, or with a blade that does not provide a smooth-enough cut surface, save the layout line and sand down all cut edges. Constant-tension saws usually cut so smooth that no or little sanding is needed. Therefore, you can usually cut right on the layout line, removing it as you saw along. This eliminates the need to sand off the layout line later.

If very precise cutting is required, the thickness and accuracy of the layout lines become more important, and the cut is normally made very close to line, but not so close that you cut it away. With practice you'll be able to split layout lines if you wish.

On-the-Spot-Turns and Cornering

On-the-spot turns and cornering are also skills that require practice. They can only be done on constant-tension saws. An on-the-spot-turn is the ability to actually spin the workpiece 360° on a very small radius that is actually just ½ of the blade width. This can be done when cutting thick or thin stock.

Spinning the workpiece around on the blade is a new experience and technique for woodworkers accustomed to conventional rigid-arm saws or band-sawing techniques. Instead of making the "spin" (turn) slowly, which is the usual way, hold down on the work while turning it as quickly as you can. Don't become alarmed if the first time or so the blade catches in the workpiece and chatters up and down on the table.

Practice 180° on-the-spot turning as shown in Illus. 90–92 until you can do it with confidence. The ability to make on-the-spot turns permits sawing sharp inside or outside corner cuts nonstop.

An example of a job requiring two sharp inside corner cuts is shown in Illus. 93. The cuts are made nonstop from start to finish. Illus. 94 is a good example of a cutout made utilizing to full advantage the on-the-spot cornering capabilities of a constant-tension scroll saw.

Illus. 95–97 show how the project depicted in Illus. 94 would be cut if you used a wide blade. As you can see in the illustrations, an on-the-spot turn is impossible with a wide blade. Notice how the outside corners are cut in Illus. 95; Illus. 95 also shows how to start an inside corner cut. Backing up, rounding the corner, and continuing the cut are shown in Illus. 96. The rounded corner is "cleaned-up" later. (See Illus. 97.) A good practice project is the "magic belt hook" shown in Illus. 98.

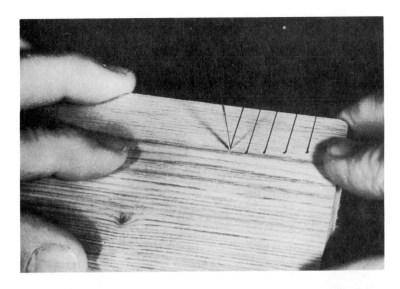

Illus. 90. Practicing "on-the-spot" turning on a constant-tension saw. To do this, saw partway into the board, spin it quickly around, and exit in the same cut (kerf).

Illus. 91. Making an on-the-spot turn, about halfway through a 180° turn.

Illus. 92. When the turn is completed, the blade should exit through the "inbound" kerf.

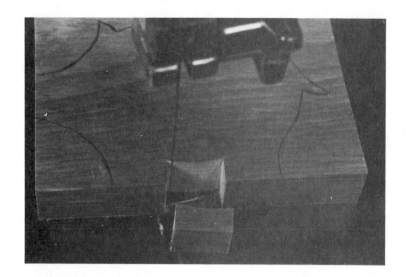

Illus. 93. The ability to make perfect 90° turns and other sharp cornering cuts accurately is the key to quick, precise and pleasurable sawing.

Illus. 94. Sharp, accurate, and quick cornering completes this cutout in just seconds.

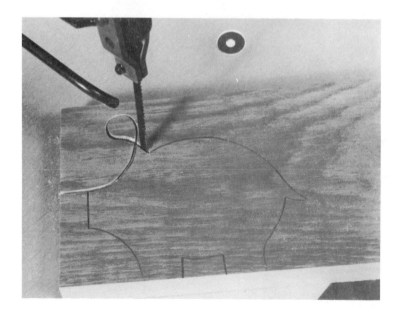

Illus. 95. Wide-blade cornering. Looping around to cut a sharp outside corner makes only the point of the ear. The blade will not make the required sharp inside corner.

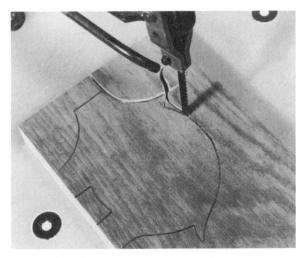

Illus. 96. Wide-blade cornering continued. Back up and "round out" the inside corner, as shown.

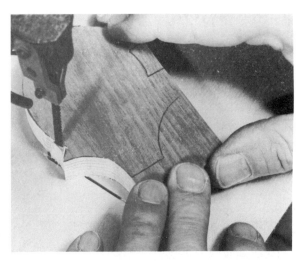

Illus. 97. Later, the inside corner is completed by cutting in from the opposite direction.

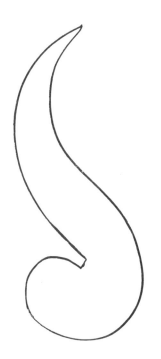

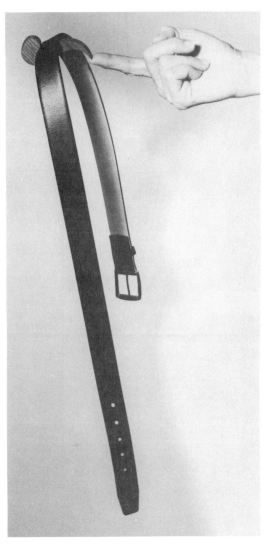

Illus. 98. This full-size pattern of the "magic belt hook" is a good practice project. Use ¼- to ⅜-inch thick material.

Straight-Line Cutting

Straight-line cutting across the grain and with the grain takes practice; also, a couple of factors have to be taken into consideration. First, almost all scroll saw and fret saw blades don't saw straight or cut parallel to the blade; they often cut a few degrees more towards one side than the other. This is because when the teeth are formed in manufacturing by milling, punching or filing, there is a material flow in one direction only, leaving a little burr remaining on one side of the teeth. This burr is much like the burr you get when grinding a new chisel or plane bevel. It makes the saw grab slightly in one direction. There is nothing the manufacturers can do about it without adding substantially to the price of blades.

When you stand facing the direct front of the saw, you will note that the angle of normal feed is off approximately 2 to 4 degrees to compensate.

You can verify this for yourself. Draw some lines across a board with a square. (See Illus. 99 .) Now cut each one on the line; you will soon determine that it's easiest to follow the line with the work feed slightly angled into the saw blade. When you understand the concept and compensate correctly, straight-line sawing freehand is surprisingly easy—even when using very narrow blades.

Straight-line ripping (sawing with the grain) is done in essentially the same way. (See Illus. 100.) However, be alert because the blade may follow the grain rather than the layout line, as you expect. In such cases, slow the feed and compensate by changing the feed angle slightly more in the appropriate direction. The toaster tongs shown in Illus. 101–103 are a good project on which to practice straight-line ripping. Use ¾-inch-thick straight-grain hardwood and finish it with peanut oil.

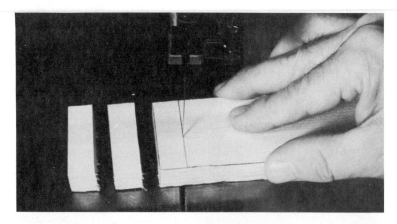

Illus. 99. Straight-line crosscutting requires a compensating, slightly angular feed direction.

Illus. 100. Straight-line cutting with the grain (ripping).

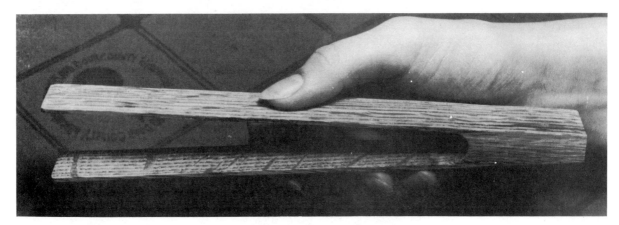

Illus. 101–103. These toaster tongs make a good straight-line sawing project.

Illus. 102.

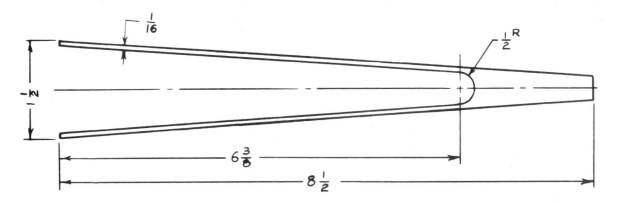

Illus. 103.

Stack Cutting

Stack cutting saves lots of time when two or more pieces need to be cut from the same pattern. Simply stack the pieces together and cut all the layers together at one time, just as you would saw one piece. The pattern only has to be marked out on the top layer. The layers of individual pieces can be held together easily with double-faced tape (Illus. 104), or you can nail into the scrap area.

It's important that the saw table be set perfectly square to the table. If it is not, some pieces will turn out larger or smaller than the others. Also, you cannot stack to a height that exceeds the thickness-cutting capacity of the saw. If the stock thickness capacity is 1½ inches, then you can stack six pieces of material ¼ inch in thickness (Illus. 105–107), but only two pieces that are ¾ inch thick.

Illus. 104. Layers are held together with small pieces of double-faced tape.

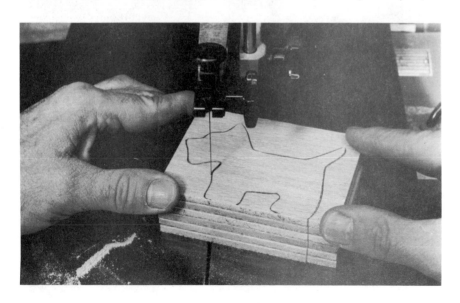

Illus. 105. Whenever two or more identical pieces are required, stack them together and cut them as one piece. Here six pieces are cut at once. (See Illus. 106 on the next page.)

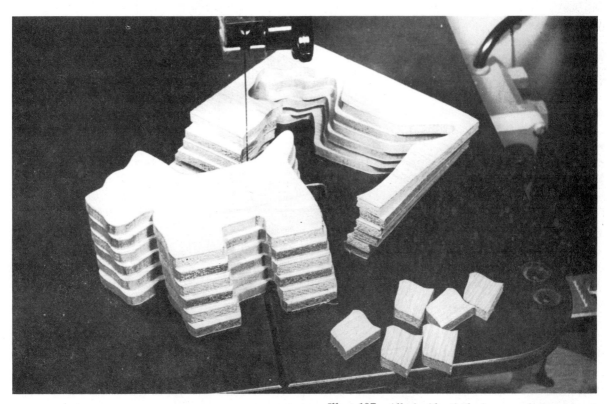

Illus. 107. All six identical pieces made in one cut.

7

PATTERNS AND PROJECTS

Good scroll saw work requires patterns of interesting and varied designs and projects. This book contains over 200 traceable project patterns designed for scroll saw use, which are given on pages 102–222. Sears has products for the layout of signs of various sizes and styles in which the layout systems are already developed. Sears Models 25196 and 25176 are sign layout kits that are available for use with the scroll saw through the Sears catalog.

COPYING AND TRANSFERRING PATTERNS

Good scroll-sawing skills hinge on the careful and accurate development of the design or pattern and the transfer of it to the wood. Most plans in magazines and project books are not full size. They are usually printed, considerably less than full size, on a two-dimensional, squared grid.

Drawing talent is not required to develop a good pattern by enlargement (or reduction) and transferring it to the wood. Even pictures and designs from books, magazines, newspapers, coloring books, napkins, wallpaper, etc., can be converted rather easily to a scroll saw pattern. Any design is possible to copy, even it is not drawn with a two-dimensional squared grid over it.

To copy and enlarge designs from such sources, begin with some transparent tissue paper. Accurately rule it out making small,

uniformly sized squares all over it in the ¼-inch or ½-inch size. The greater the detail and the smaller the design being copied, the smaller the size of the squares should be drawn. Next, on a larger piece of paper, about the size that you want the eventual project design to be, divide the space up with exactly the same number of squares as occupied by the design under the transparent tissue paper. The size of the larger set of squares can also be determined by the enlargement ratio desired. If you want the design twice the size, then draw the big squares twice the size of the smaller ones.

Now, copy the design square by square. Copy each point of the original pattern onto the graph squares. Curves may be drawn by "eye" after locating them with reference to their surrounding square. However, it is more accurate to mark the points where the line of the curve strikes each horizontal and vertical line, as shown in Illus. 108. The example shown in Illus. 108 has a 1 to 4 ratio, which means the design is enlarged four times larger than the original.

This technique can be modified so that the design is drawn directly onto the surface of the wood if so desired. Usually, however, the pattern is drawn onto paper first. It's easier to erase, refine, and smooth out contoured lines. When the full-size paper pattern is made, you have several choices of how to transfer the pattern to the wood.

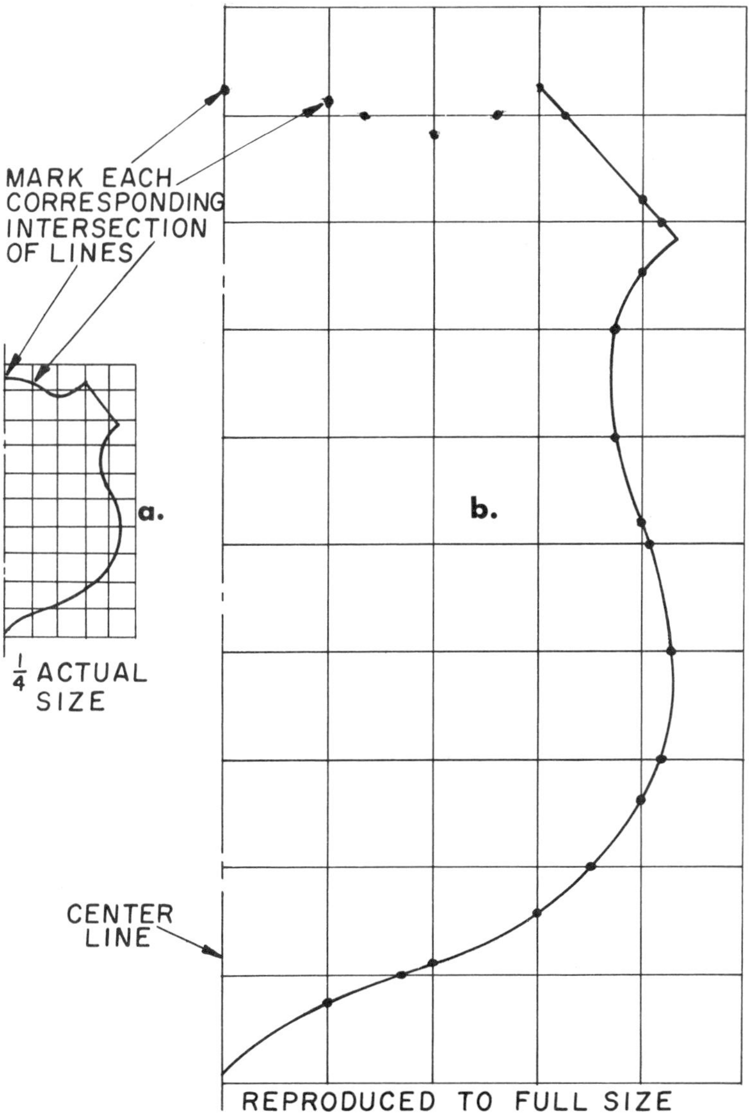

MARK EACH
CORRESPONDING
INTERSECTION
OF LINES

a.

b.

$\frac{1}{4}$ ACTUAL
SIZE

CENTER
LINE

REPRODUCED TO FULL SIZE

Illus. 108. Enlarging a design pattern with the graph square or grid system. A is the original design; B shows the method of locating the points for the enlarged pattern.

Sometimes you might decide to paste the entire pattern directly onto the workpiece. Rubber cement seems the best for this because it does not wrinkle the paper and rubs off fairly easily. For highly detailed precision-cutting, as when making jewellery, miniatures, gears, etc., scissor-cut the pattern out and glue it to the workpiece with rubber cement. This gives a very crisp, sharp line that's highly visible, accurate, and much easier to follow than any other line. The disadvantage of this technique is that you must sacrifice the pattern; it cannot be reused. Also, it's not always fast or easy to remove the pattern and rubber cement from the work surface.

The design can also be transferred to the workpiece with carbon paper, as shown Illus. 109 and 110. Still another method is to enlarge the pattern onto a piece of heavier paper (like a file folder) or lightweight cardboard (like a writing tablet "backer"). Then, cut out the pattern with scissors. Place it on the workpiece and trace around it with a pencil, as shown in Illus. 111. This method is probably the best in that it least dirties or soils the surface, thus requiring less subsequent sanding.

Another method that has some applications is the transfer of the pattern to the wood with a pounce wheel. (See Illus. 112.)

On light wood, you can put carbon paper underneath. On softwoods you can just exert enough pressure to track in the wood. This method is not recommended for projects requiring accuracy. It's best to cut the wood with the blade, actually removing the depressions left by this marking tool.

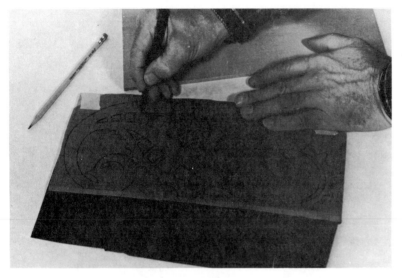

Illus. 109. The enlarged design is drawn on heavy paper and transferred to the wood with carbon paper.

Illus. 110. The pattern transferred to the wood. Since two pieces will be required, one ¼ inch wider than the other, for a butt corner shelf joint, the pieces are offset and secured with double-faced tape so they both can be cut to the same shape at one time.

Illus. 111. Tracing around a scissor-cut pattern made of heavy paper.

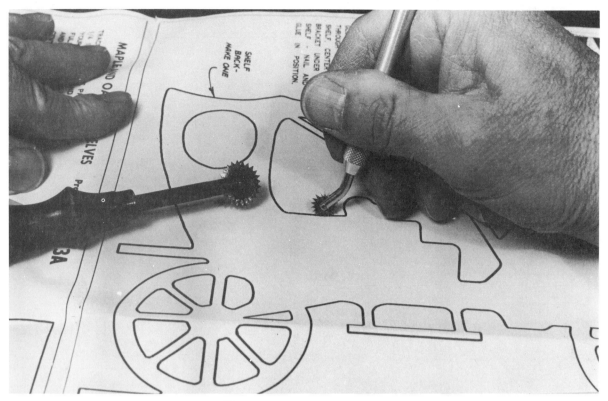

Illus. 112. Transferring a pattern with a pounce wheel or tracing wheel.

Using a Pantograph

A pantograph is still another way of copying any two-dimensional or flat profile shape. (See Illus. 113.) The enlargement (or reduction) can be drawn directly onto the workpiece or onto paper. The follower point is guided along the original design as the pencil end automatically recreates the outline in the exact size and desired proportions.

Office Copy Machines

Office copy machines are also very useful to the scroll saw craftsman. Some even have the capabilities to enlarge or reduce, which, for the cost of one copy, is certainly very reasonable. Usually, the simplest designs are easy to visualize in terms of a scroll-saw project. With experience, you will be able to visualize more and more potential project designs. Illus. 114–117 depict a project developed simply from a 1-to-1 copy taken from a book on birds.

COMMERCIAL PATTERNS

Commercial patterns have been around for a long time. (See Illus. 118–120.) A look at the advertising pages in the popular woodcraft magazines will uncover many sources for plans and patterns. Sears stores have a fairly inexpensive sign layout pattern kit. (See Illus. 121–123.) The kit contains 100 patterns in script, Old English, and block letter styles in 2-, 3-, and 4-inch letter sizes. To use, transfer the patterns to the wood with carbon paper. The patterns are designed so that proper spacing is easy to achieve as the wording is progressively developed. (See Illus. 122 and 123.)

Since sign work is a popular activity for scroll saw owners, I recommend the two sign layout kits (Models #25196 and 25176) available through the Sears catalog. Both products include stencils, carbon and a plastic carbon cover. The stencils are 3–5″ and 6–10″ in height.

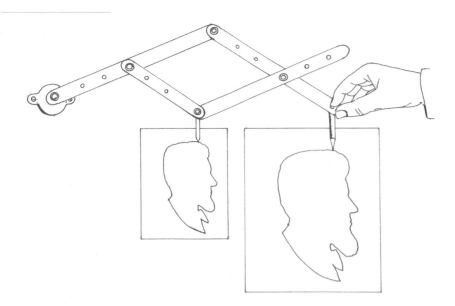

Illus. 113. An inexpensive pantograph (less than $7.00) enlarges a pattern to over 10 times its original size or reduces it to 1/10 its original size.

Illus. 114. This book page was copied on a Xerox machine.

Illus. 115. The copy was pasted to the back of 1/4-inch veneer plywood with rubber cement. Two layers of plywood were secured face to face with just two small pieces of double-faced tape near the edges. Here is the cutting in progress.

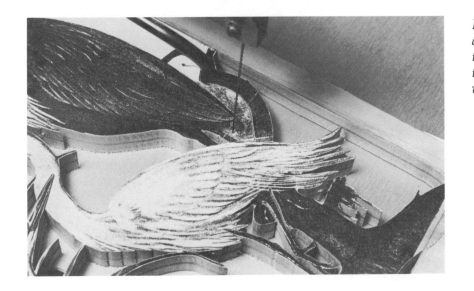

Illus. 116. A close-up look at the cutting. Remember, the copy (pattern) is pasted to the back side of one workpiece.

Illus. 117. The resulting delicate silhouette projects. Anywhere from three to six silhouettes can be made at one time if a precision saw is used.

Illus. 118. The "Pattern Pack" is a rather expensive subscription service.

Illus. 119. A typical full-size pattern from the "Pattern Pack."

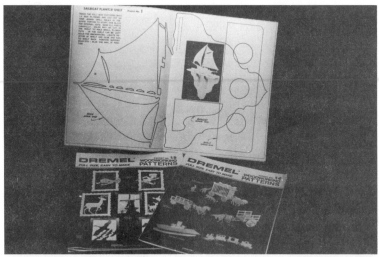

Illus. 120. A typical full-size scroll-saw project packet sold by Dremel.

Illus. 121. The sign layout kit sold by Sears consists of two-, three-, and four-inch patterns for alphabets in script, Old English, and block letter designs.

Illus. 122. The board needs a length-wise center line.

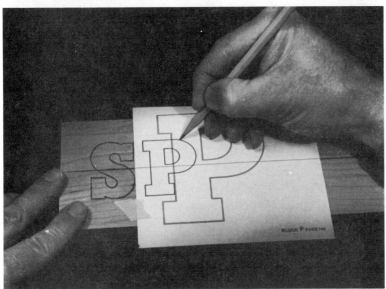

Illus. 123. If the letters are to be connected, like those used for a desk sign, the spacing between them is the distance the letter is from the left edge of the paper.

Illus. 124. Some basic sign project ideas.

Illus. 125 and 126. Hanging-lamp projects require a combination of techniques: namely, stack-cutting and sawing inside openings. Full-size patterns for these projects can be found on pages 211–214.

TEMPLATES

Templates are ideal when two or more identical layouts are required. (See Illus. 127.) A template is nothing more than a full-size pattern cut from a stiff, rigid material that can be easily traced around. Almost any thin, inexpensive sheet material can be used for making templates. One-eighth-inch tempered hardboard, thin plywood, sheet aluminum, thin plastics, etc., can all be used. *Tip*: If you have already made a paper pattern or the design is already transferred to the wood, and you decide that it would be nice to have a permanent template, cut one on your saw simultaneously as you cut out your project. Use double-faced tape to attach the template material under the workpiece. It takes just a little effort to produce a perfect copy template while cutting out the first project(s).

PROJECT IDEAS

Jigsaw Puzzles

Jigsaw puzzles are very easy and fun to make. (See Illus. 130.) Simply find a suitable picture, perhaps from a calendar, magazine, or poster shop. Bond it to ⅛-inch-thick hardboard with rubber cement. Apply two coats to each surface; allow the first coat to dry completely before applying the second coat. (See Illus. 131.) With chalk, roughly mark out the sizes of the pieces desired. If you want a more complicated puzzle, plan to cut it into more and smaller pieces. Cut bigger and fewer pieces for younger children's puzzles. Make the typical interlocking puzzle cuts freehand, using the chalked guidelines for piece and size reference only. (See Illus. 132.) Make all the cuts in one direction first, as shown in Illus. 132. Lay the cut strips, assembled together, onto a piece of corrugated box cardboard. Then make the second run of cuts in the opposite direction, as shown in Illus. 133. The cardboard supports the pieces until they are cut away.

Decorative Wall Puzzles

Decorative wall puzzles are also fun to make with the scroll saw. (See Illus. 134.) Pictures, photos, etc., are stylized and reduced to represent simple pictorial lines and shapes. The puzzle shown in Illus. 135—

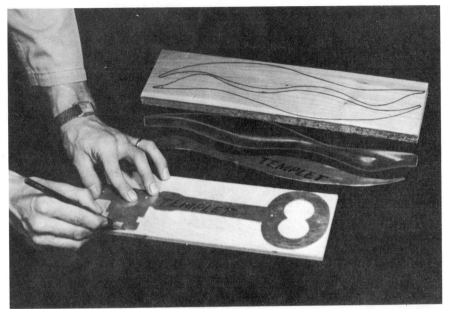

Illus. 127. Marking the wood with templates cut from an aluminum sheet. As you may notice in the illustration, the word template can be spelled two different ways.

Illus. 128. These commercial letter templates of clear plastic come in a variety of styles and sizes. They are available from Sevco Sales Co.

Illus. 129. Tracing around the plastic letter templates.

Illus. 130. A jigsaw puzzle is a fun, easy-to-make project for beginners.

Illus. 131. A suitable picture, ⅛-inch-thick hardboard, and rubber cement are needed to make a jigsaw puzzle.

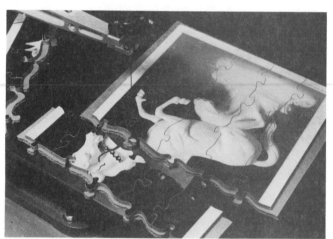

Illus. 133. Once the vertical puzzle cuts are made, assemble them on a piece of cardboard. Hold the puzzle stock and cardboard together with hand pressure and make the horizontal, interlocking cuts.

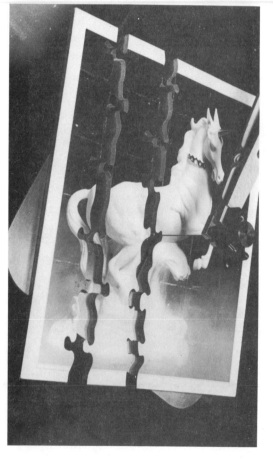

Illus. 132. Light, grid chalk lines are used to indicate the relative sizes and maintain some uniformity during cutting. The interlocking cuts are made freehand without any precise layout lines.

"Lovers in the Moonlight"—is from a commercial plan and is available from Advanced Machinery Imports, Box 312, New Castle, Delaware 19720. However, you can create your own patterns for stylized works of scroll-sawing art. Cut out individual pieces on the layout lines. Use ¾-inch or thicker stock. Cut out an uninterrupted border piece and glue it to a thin plywood backing. (See Illus. 135 and 136.) Sand every individual piece on the top edge, just to round the edges slightly. Individually stain or paint all of the cutout parts in contrasting colors or tones; combining stain and pigmented colors in the same project leads to a very nice-looking puzzle. Then, either leave the parts free or glue them to the backing. The stock lost from kerf made by the fine blade makes a shadow line, giving a feeling of depth to the project.

Illus. 135. The border is glued to a backing and the edges of all cut parts are softened and slightly rounded with sandpaper.

Illus. 134. AMI's "Lovers in the Moonlight" is a decorative wall puzzle.

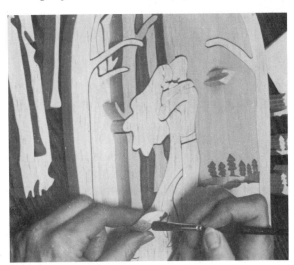

Illus. 136. Individually stain and paint all cutout pieces in contrasting colors. Glue them to the backing.

8
SAWING INSIDE OPENINGS

Sawing inside openings—sometimes called piercing work, pierce cutting, or internal cutting—is not only a common procedure, but a frequently utilized one as well. (See Illus. 137–141.) In this class of scroll-sawing work, the blade is threaded through a hole drilled into the workpiece. The detail or design of the pattern is cut as usual, and then the blade is unclamped and removed. This is a relatively uncomplicated sawing procedure.

The complexity of the overall project and the number of openings that must be cut, dictate the time involved and the number of blade threadings required for a given project. [For example, fretwork, which is often more highly detailed, with a very large percentage of delicate cutouts making up the overall design, takes relatively more time and blade threadings than other projects.] Illus. 137 and 138 represent two typical extremes. The seahorse designs in Illus. 137 will require a great number of blade manipulations. The cat cutouts in Illus. 138 do not.

To saw out each opening, repeat the following general steps: 1) release the blade tension, 2) unclamp the blade, 3) thread the blade through the predrilled workpiece, 4) reclamp the blade, and 5) retension. Some scroll saws require a great deal more time and effort to complete these simple steps than do other saws.

The essential differences between making internal cutouts with constant-tension and the rigid-arm saws are shown in Illus. 142–144.

Illus. 137. Here is a sample of work that requires a high percentage of inside cutouts.

74

Illus. 138. When an inside pattern is cut on a constant-tension saw with a thin, narrow blade, useful "positive" and "negative" pieces can be made.

Illus. 139. These narrow cutouts are being made with a constant-tension saw.

Illus. 140. The completed project. Designs like this can be used for signboards or other projects.

75

Illus. 142. Threading a blade for an inside cut on a rigid-arm scroll saw. Note the blade width.

Illus. 141. A small, inexpensive spiral drill.

Illus. 143. Making an inside cut on thick stock with a rigid-arm saw. Remember, the size of the "turning holes" equals the outline of the cut.

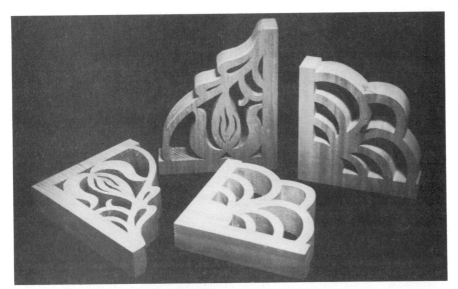

Illus. 144. Heavy brackets cut from 1¾- and 2-inch-thick stock in cedar and oak challenge the maximum capabilities of the scroll saw.

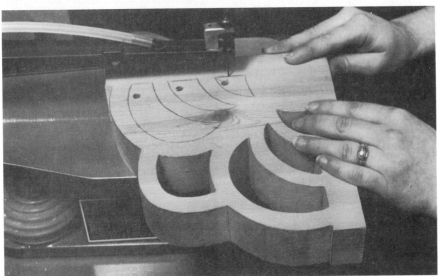

Illus. 145. Making inside cuts on 1¾-inch-thick stock with a constant-tension saw.

Illus. 146. A very narrow blade was used to make the inside cuts on the line comprising this signature; the cuts were made through ¾-inch oak.

9
SAWING SMALL PIECES AND THIN STOCK

Sawing thin wood or soft metallic pieces, as done in jewellery making, is work that can be perfectly handled with a good scroll saw. Illus. 147–150 show the essentials of do-it-yourself jewellery making. Pieces even smaller than those depicted can be cut on the scroll saw. Minute items for miniatures and scale-model projects are also easily handled on the scroll saw.

This class of work can best be done more safely on a scroll saw more than any other machine. However, anytime you are working very small pieces on a machine, extra precautions should be taken. Very small cuttings often dictate that you get your fingers in very close to the blade. (See Illus. 149.) You'll most likely be working with thinner and narrower blades, which break more frequently. So, be aware of potential hazards and don't let your concentration lapse. Select the appropriate blade and tension it accordingly.

Fine and highly detailed designs might be more easily cut with a slower speed setting to reduce the number of cutting strokes per minute. If sawing a considerable amount of thinner material, adjust your machine to a shorter-than-usual stroke length if your machine is able to do this. Shorter cutting strokes increase efficiency and accuracy when cutting thin materials.

Illus. 147. Do-it-yourself jewelry can be easily made on the scroll saw.

Illus. 148. Rubber cement is used for pasting scissor-cut patterns to the workpieces. Double-faced tape is used for multiple stack cutting.

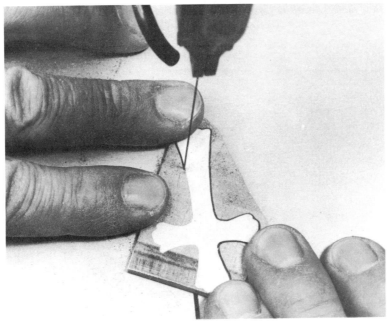

Illus. 149. A close-up showing the sawing of soft brass. The paper pattern glued to the material makes a precise cutting line.

Illus. 150. Jewelry findings are simply glued on with epoxy.

SAWING EXTREMELY SMALL PIECES

Illus. 151 and 152 show how to saw extremely small pieces. One of the problems associated with cutting out very small pieces is the table opening around the blade. (See Illus. 151.) Some machines have larger blade openings than others. The openings must be at least a certain size to permit the table to be tilted without the blade striking the table. Thus, when cutting small pieces, there is a lack of support in the opening. This causes small pieces to tip in or fall through; thin material can bend, tear, or break because it is not supported at the blade area.

This problem can be overcome in one of two ways or a combination of both. One technique is to saw the material while it is supported on another piece of waste material. Cheap plywood or a flat piece of corrugated cardboard may do the trick. (See Illus. 152.) The other method is to use an auxiliary table made of thin plywood or hardboard. This is cut to an appropriate size, and a very small hole is drilled for the blade opening. Thread the blade through the small hole and secure the auxiliary table to the original table with double-faced tape. (See Illus. 153.) Sometimes the nature of the job is such that both methods are utilized. An example would be cutting out a small design from thin veneer.

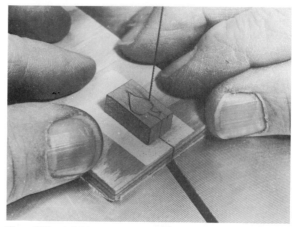

Illus. 152. *Making a very small cutout. The workpiece is secured to a scrap piece of plywood with double-faced tape. This way, the work is supported and your fingers do not have to be close to the moving blade.*

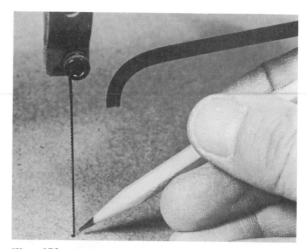

Illus. 153. *This auxiliary table of hardboard is attached to the existing table with double-faced tape. Note the small hole at the blade so that the workpiece will have sufficient support.*

Some very delicate and unusual projects can be made with mini-cutouts. Various designs for overlays, jewellery, miniatures, and model-building of extremely small profile shapes can be cut from a variety of thin materials. One project idea is to make little "stick-on" designs from veneer scraps. Apply double-faced tape to the back before sawing out the part and you can adhere little veneer cutouts to almost any surface, including very smooth plastic and glass. Or simply use the new "peel and stick" veneers that already have adhesive applied to one side.

Illus. 151. *This mini-cutout was sawn while supported on a piece of scrap plywood. You can visualize the problem presented by the blade opening on the table unless some auxiliary support for the work is provided.*

10

BEVEL SAWING, AND INLAY, RELIEF, AND RECESSING WORK

Bevel sawing involves any one of the wide range of cutting jobs that are performed with the saw table tilted. Inlays and some forms of marquetry could be included in this category, and sections are devoted to these subjects. Bevel sawing is also done on the scroll saw to make the "pins" of dovetail joints.

Bevel-sawing operations allow for some creative scroll-sawing projects, but this class of work is not easily performed on all scroll saws. Some saws do not have any table-tilting features. Others have tilting features that may present some serious problems, even preventing some bevel-sawing work from being performed at all. Therefore, the bevel-sawing capacities of a scroll saw will be enhanced considerably if the scroll saw has good table-tilting functions and a blade that cuts thick pieces.

One important point to note: when a bevel is sawed with the table tilted, the cut is being made through more material than just the normal thickness of the workpiece. For example, a board that's ¾ of an inch in normal thickness presents about 1⅛ inches of material for cutting when it is fed to the blade at a 45° tilt.

MAKING CUTOUTS

Almost any cutout can be sawed with the table tilted. However, bevel sawing is one area of scroll sawing in which the amount of detail in the shape dictates how accurately and "cleanly" the object can be cut. Increasing the amount of tilt or bevel, coupled with progressively greater detailing that involves sharp inside corners, proportionally reduces the capabilities of bevel sawing.

A relatively simple disc or doughnut shape, such as the letter "o," can be cut easily with 45° edges if desired. This is because there are no sharp inside corners on a letter "o," and the curve is fairly consistent regardless of its size. Any cutouts having an extremely small radius or sharp inside corners will create some very serious problems when cut on-the-bevel. Illus. 154 and 155 show this problem with the example of the Old-English style letter "s" that has been bevel-cut on a tilted table.

Illus. 156 shows random bevel cutting on the sides of a hexagon hanging lamp. With the cuts made at various widths, varying amounts of light shine through the lamp.

Illus. 154. In bevel sawing, the wood is cut while supported on a tilted table. This produces the bevelled edges on the letters shown here. Inside corners, shown at the right, will not cut cleanly. See Illus. 155.

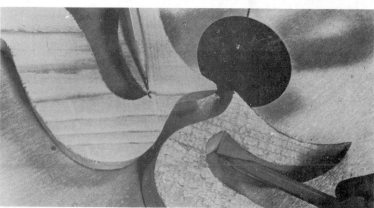

Illus. 155. A close look at the results of sharp inside cornering when bevel sawing. The little kerfs cut into the edges (back and front) cannot be eliminated unless the corners are cut on a radius, rather than sharply—as done here.

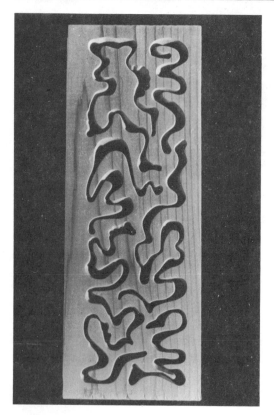

Illus. 156. A side panel for a hexagon lamp. The irregular lines were bevel-cut to varying widths, which permits a variable amount of light to shine through—making this a very interesting project.

ON-THE-SPOT-TURNS

When an on-the-spot turn is made in stock supported on a tilted table, the result is a cone-shaped piece that comes out of the bottom or the downside. (See Illus. 158.) Practice a few of these cuts on scrap pieces, trying both clockwise and counterclockwise turning directions. With the table tilted to the left, you'll probably find it easier to make the turn feeding the stock in one direction rather than the other. The reverse will be true with the table tilted in the opposite direction. This will be helpful to you when bevel-cutting some fairly detailed designs.

INCISED BEVEL-CUT SIGNS

Making incised bevel-cut signs, as shown in Illus. 159, is another unusual application of bevel sawing. This type of cutting calls for skills similar to bevel on-the-spot turning. A certain amount of "kerfing-in" at some corners, along with a little burning, is to be expected on some surfaces. The density of the wood species selected may have some influence on the level of cutting difficulty for this type of bevel sawing. Butternut, ¾ of an inch thick, was used for the sign shown in Illus. 159.

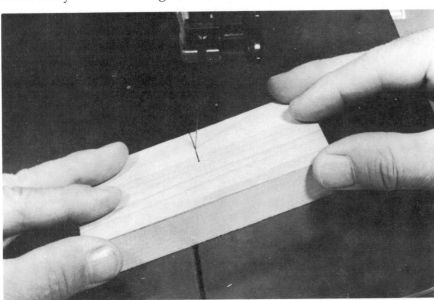

Illus. 157 "Backing out" after making an on-the-spot-turn with the table tilted for bevel sawing. See Illus. 158.

Illus. 158. Here's the result: a perfect cone-shaped dimple cut into the bottom surface.

Illus. 159. An example of the type of incised bevel-cut signs that can be cut on the scroll saw. Note the scraps in the foreground.

Select a fine blade and drill the smallest possible hole at an outside corner of each letter for blade threading. (See Illus. 160.) The angles of the drilling and the sawing must be fairly close to equal. The angle for sawing of stock ¾ inches thick can vary from 14 to 18°. This will give approximately a ½- to ⅝-inch width at the face of the letter when the V cut is made all the way into the thickness of the board. To determine the maximum width for the letters, just make an on-the-spot turn in a scrap piece of the same thickness and measure the diameter at the base of the cone-shaped piece. Lay out the letter patterns on the workpiece with the widest part of any letter not exceeding the diameter of the cone produced by a bevelled on-the-spot turn.

The scrap test piece used for the on-the-spot turn can be cut in half and used as a drilling guide. (See Illus. 160.) This will ensure that the holes are drilled at the same angle the table is tilted to. It's best to drill the blade-threading holes at outside corners rather than inside ones.

When all the holes are drilled, thread the blade through the workpiece and begin sawing. *Caution*: Make sure you feed the stock so that the slant of the letter face is towards the center. With the table tilted left, the letter is cut out by sawing clockwise around the letter. Also, make the cut on very sharp turns by spinning the workpiece in a clockwise di-rection. Always make every sharp turn (both inside and outside ones) with the stock moving in a clockwise direction. (See Illus. 161.) This means that on some turns you will have to rotate the work almost 360° to stay on the line.

The techniques will obviously require some study and practice, but the results are impressive and unusual. (Illus. 163 shows a back view of the completed sign.)

Illus. 160. Drilling holes at an angle for threading the blade. The guide block helps to drill at the proper angle. The block itself is half a piece of scrap used for the on-the-spot turn with the table tilted to the desired angle.

Illus. 161. Making bevel-sawn incise-lettering cutouts. The point of the "r" being cut here is best made with a clockwise feed. That will mean making almost a full 360° on-the-spot turn to go around this "point" of the letter.

Illus. 162. Here is the intact waste from the letter "r".

Illus. 163. A rear view of the sign shown in Illus. 159. Note that all of the cone-shaped cutouts are located where clockwise on-the-spot turns were made to complete very sharp cornering cuts.

SOLID WOOD INLAYS

The objective in solid wood inlay is to fit the pieces so tightly together that no space at all exists in the joint line. Even the thinnest and smallest fret blades will leave undesirable kerf spaces or cracks between the fitted pieces. This space can be eliminated entirely by tilting the table slightly, somewhere between one to eight or ten degrees for making the cuts.

Illus. 164 shows the relationship of the variables involved when solid wood inlays are bevel-sawed. The variables that must be coordinated are the blade width, the stock thicknesses, and the preferred angle of table tilt. Because the background stock and the inlay material are cut simultaneously, as in stack-cutting, the two pieces must be temporarily fastened together. This can be accomplished by using a little rubber cement, masking tape, a drop of hot-melt glue, or what I often prefer—small pieces of double-faced tape.

Trial and error is the easiest way to determine the optimum amount of table tilt that is suitable for the blade width and stock thickness being used. If you change blade widths or material thickness between jobs, the saw table will have to be readjusted. For a flush inlay, the opening of the bevel-cut background has to be equal to that of the bevel-cut inlay. This is shown in Illus. 165. The results desired in making the flush inlay are shown in Illus. 166.

Illus. 167–172 show the step-by-step procedures for making a simple flush heart inlay. However, before starting, make sure you have a scroll saw that can produce a perfectly straight and true cut surface in the combined thickness of the two pieces that require cutting. If there is any "belly"-like bulges or the blade drifts and wanders, all of your efforts will be wasted. Also, use fine blades so the threading hole will be as small as possible. The blade must be tensioned sufficiently to obtain a true cut, which means that initially blades will break more frequently. However, eventually you will work out a satisfactory compromise.

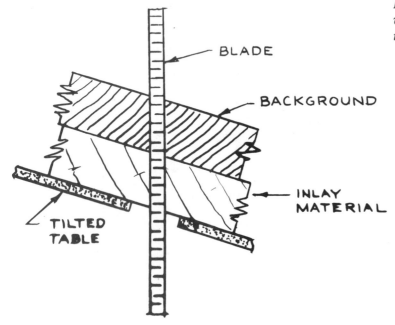

Illus. 164. The relationship of the various factors involved in bevel sawing solid inlay material.

BLADE

BACKGROUND

INLAY MATERIAL

TILTED TABLE

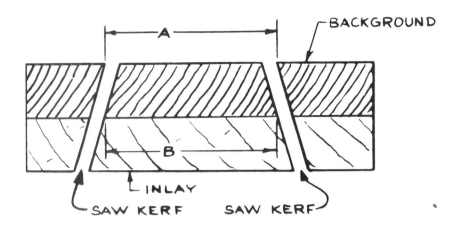

Illus. 165. When the correct table tilt angle is used for sawing, the distance of "a" will be exactly equal to that of "b."

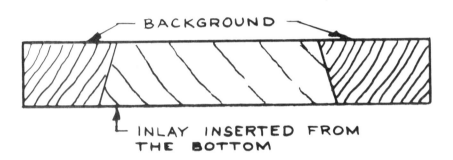

Illus. 166. This flush bevel-cut solid-wood inlay is an absolutely perfect fit; no saw kerf spaces are visible.

Illus. 167. Begin with two scrap pieces of stock equal to the thickness of the proposed workpieces. Tape them together for a test cut to check for the correct table tilt adjustment.

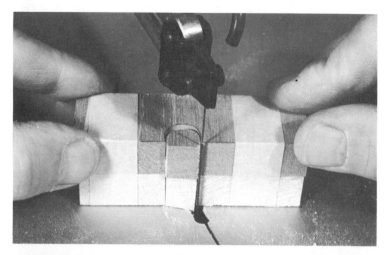

Illus. 168. Making the test cut. A simple circular cut, as shown, is sufficient.

Illus. 169. When the angle of the cut is correct, the upper piece will slip snugly into the lower cutout.

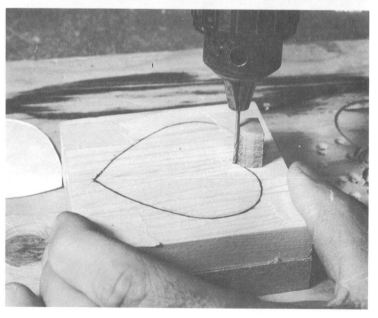

Illus. 170. Use the scrap test piece to help line up the correct drill angle for blade threading. The hole location is selected at a less conspicuous inside corner. The workpieces are arranged for a bottom inserted inlay with the light wood going into the background of darker wood. The cut will be made with the workpiece rotated clockwise into the blade. If the cut is made in a counterclockwise feed direction, the slant would bevel outward, and you will have the dark piece inlaying the light piece with a top insertion.

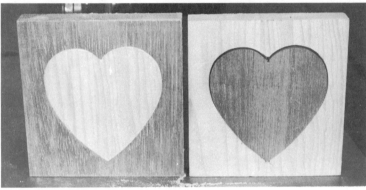

Illus. 172. The flush inlay on the left is completed. The scrap pieces on the right will be thrown away.

The stacking arrangement of the two pieces and the direction that you feed the workpiece into the blade have to be thought out before you drill the blade hole, as shown in Illus. 170. The way you drill the hole and the way you feed the material into the blade (clockwise or counterclockwise) will determine if the inlay will fit into the background piece the way you planned it to. (See Illus. 171 and 172.)

The inlay can be planned and cut out so it will either be inserted from the bottom or it is inserted into the background piece from the top. Either way is perfectly acceptable as long as you plan it that way. The top insertion is preferred if you're gluing the inlay into the background along the bevelled-cut edges. With a bottom insertion, there is a tendency for the glue to be pushed up and out on to the top face of the project. This is not desirable.

INLAYS FOR WOODTURNINGS

The procedures used for inlays for wood turnings are essentially the same procedures as those just described. (See Illus. 173–178.) Inlays are simply set into boards that are laminated or glued together to make the blank for turning. The inlaid pieces are turned as usual along with the other parts that comprise the turning. The key is careful planning with a pre-established shape and contour that best takes advantage of the inlay design. Although the inlay shown in Illus. 173–178 is on a spindle-turning project, the same idea can be applied to many types and kinds of turnings. Bowls, lidded containers, plates, etc., all can be glued together with stock having flush inlays.

Illus. 174. The test cutting block is used to check the correct table-tilt angle.

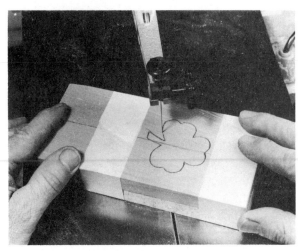

Illus. 175. Bevel sawing the inlay. The background material is on top. The material is fed counterclockwise into the blade.

Illus. 173. These pieces and layout have been selected for a laminated turning blank with flush inlays.

Illus. 176. The inlays are cut and inserted.

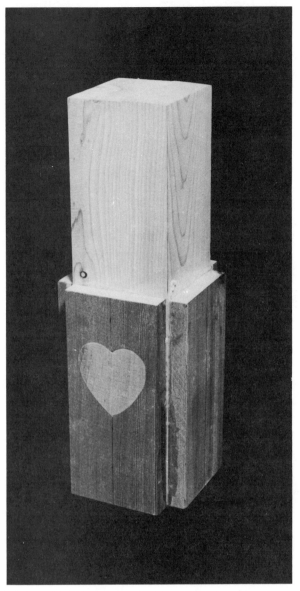

Illus. 177. The turning blank glued together.

Illus. 178. The completed turning.

SILHOUETTES

Bevel sawing to make tight fitting joinery is a procedure that can be applied whenever you want to eliminate a saw kerf. The silhouettes shown in Illus. 179–183 are good examples. The interconnected cuts fit together perfectly because the saw kerf has been eliminated in the same way flush inlays are made. Since both pieces are cut simultaneously, the margin for error has been eliminated.

The patterns for silhouettes can be enlarged from side view photos taken with an instant camera. The enlargement patterns can be made by the graph-square technique or by using a pantograph. The photos can also be enlarged on an office copier that has enlargement capabilities.

The concept of making irregular joints that are gap-free can also be applied to wood bowl and plate turnings, cutting boards, box designs, and many other projects.

Illus. 179. Interconnecting silhouettes are bevel-cut at the joint lines to make tight fits and to eliminate saw kerfs.

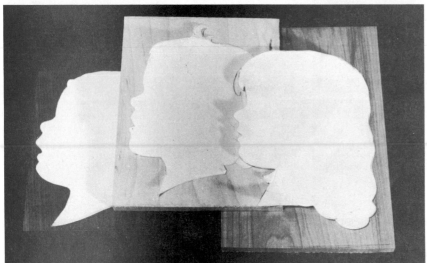

Illus. 180. Paper patterns and wood pieces of contrasting colors are selected and arranged for overlapping.

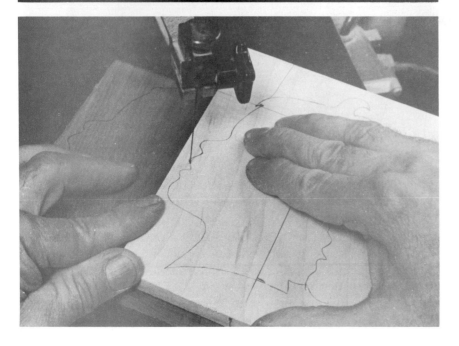

Illus. 181. When bevel sawing with one piece over the other, as in inlay sawing, hold the pieces temporarily together with double-faced tape.

92

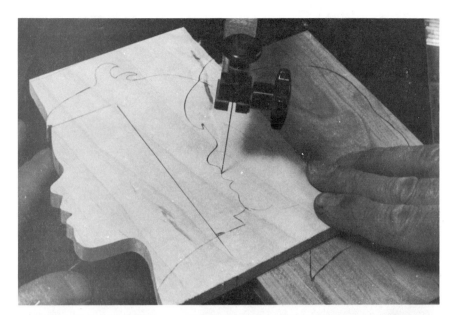

Illus. 182. Cutting the second joint in the same manner.

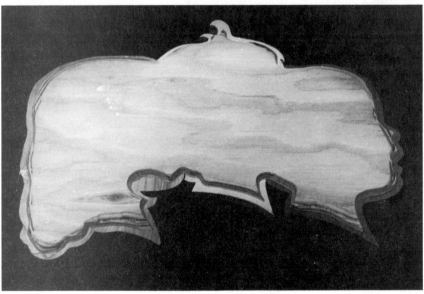

Illus. 183. This rear view shows pieces glued to a piece of plywood for reinforcement.

"SCULPTURE" INLAYS

Inlays that look like sculptures can be made by working the surfaces with contoured carving, texturing, etc. Some of the edges can even be worked or rounded over, as shown in Illus. 184–186. However, inlays with rounded-over edges tend to have deep shadows, and the tight fit produced by bevel-sawing cannot always be fully appreciated visually. For example, compare Illus. 186 and 187.

Because internal cutouts can be made using extremely thin blades that require very

small entry holes, projects such as that shown in Illus. 187 are enticing to the scroll saw user. For this class of work, the table *is not* tilted. The rounding over camouflages the kerf-spacing shadow. Interesting and attractive wall plaques similar to the one shown in Illus. 187 are possible even with the most basic design patterns. The one problem with this technique, however, is that some method must be employed to hold the reinserted cutout in place. Usually, it's glued to a thin backing board.

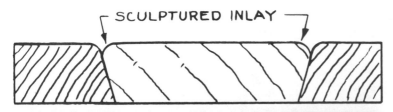

SCULPTURED INLAY

Illus. 184. The essentials of a sculptured inlay.

Illus. 185. Note the rounded-over edges on both parts.

Illus. 186. The inlay is in place, and there is no kerf spacing, just a shadow.

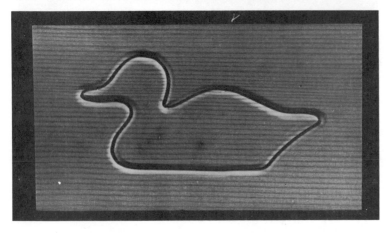

Illus. 187. This is not an inlay. It's simply a cutout with rounded-over edges. The shadow hides the saw kerf spacing. See Illus. 188.

Illus. 188 shows a bevel-sawn cutout with a sculptured look. It is not an inlay. When makin a bevel-sawn cutout, select a sawing angle that will not only close the saw kerf space, but also allows the cutout to be pushed out so it's in relief. (See Illus. 189 and 190.) Rather than attempting to make a glue line between the two bevel-sawn surfaces, simply run a fillet around the back side. Otherwise, when you glue on the edges, glue could be pushed up with the inserted piece; the result could be a messy job to clean up.

PICTURES IN RELIEF

Some especially interesting picture projects can be made by combining various techniques. (See Illus. 191–197.)

Think carefully about the table tilt and the appropriate feed direction before starting to saw out the parts. Even though the table tilt is adjusted so that the kerf can be eliminated, all of your work will be wasted if the cutout is made with the wrong feed direction of the workpiece. Determine beforehand whether the workpiece must be rotated into the blade with a clockwise or a counterclockwise stock rotation when making the cut.

Illus. 191 shows all of the pieces cut out; some of the pieces will be raised in relief. The end result is shown in Illus. 192. Small router bits can sometimes be used to round over corners. Usually, however, small pieces and parts are too small to be safely cut with the router. Use whatever means available that matches your tooling. The interesting effect of having some pieces in relief and other pieces not in relief can be further dramatized by staining individual pieces different colors. (See Illus. 197.)

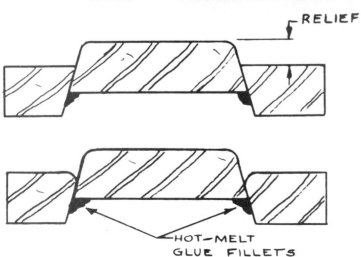

Illus. 188. This is a bevel-sawn cutout, not an inlay. The inlay bevel-cutting technique is employed to close the kerf, and the angle is such that it places the cutout in half relief to the background.

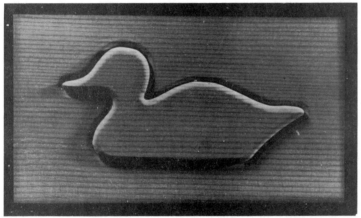

Illus. 189 and 190. When bevel-sawing for a tight relief fit, you can round some or all of the exposed corners.

Illus. 190.

95

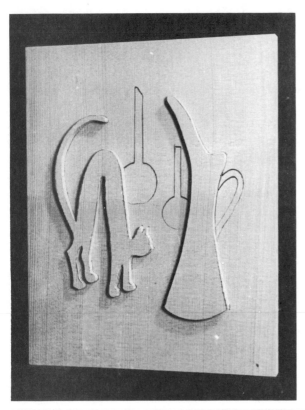

Illus. 191. A picture in relief. Some elements will be flush, and others will be raised in relief.

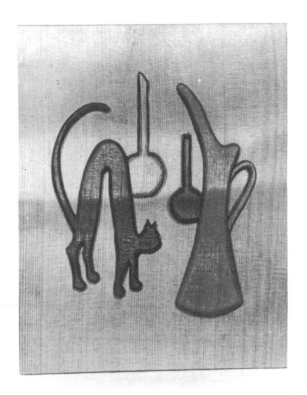

Illus. 192. Here is the final result: a combination of flush and relief pieces, all with rounded edges, that make an eye-catching project.

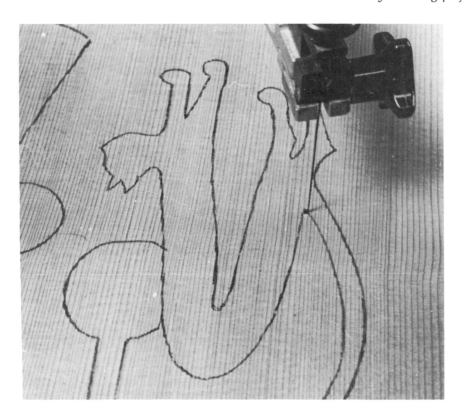

Illus. 193. This blade has been threaded for sawing. Note that the blade entry is at the sharp intersection of the tail and body. The feed direction will be clockwise into the blade with the table tilted to the left. For a raised bevel, cut in relief.

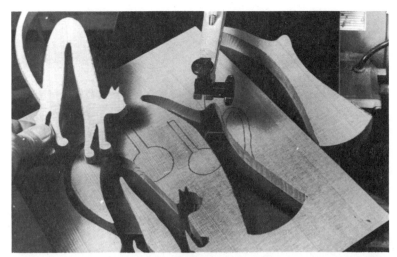

Illus. 194. All of the parts that will be in relief are cut on the bevel.

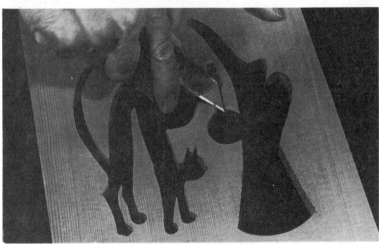

Illus. 195 and 196 (left and below). Rounding over edges with tools. Follow this procedure with sanding.

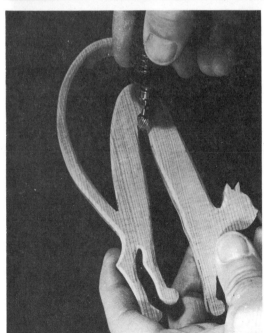

Illus. 196.

Illus. 197. Staining pieces various colors before inserting them adds interest and variety to the final project.

You can also work some designs into the background surface by setting the cutouts inward so that they are recessed. This is also achieved by bevel-sawing, as shown in Illus. 198. This technique can be used to improve the dimensional effects of signs and pictorial scenes. The recessed pieces can be taken out and stained or painted for sharp contrast and then reinserted. If the material protruding out of the opposite or back side (Illus. 199) is objectionable, it can be removed with a belt sander or hand plane.

COMBINING TECHNIQUES

Flush inlaying, relief projection, sculpturing edges, and recessing surfaces are techniques that can be combined. In addition, you can use contrasting woods in relief or recessed inlays. (See Illus. 200 and 201.) Finally, consider combining unlike materials—such as a brass inlay in some exotic hardwood as a piece of jewellery or a personalized monogram inlaid in bone or ivory on a jewellery box. Use any of the hard plastics or make the inlay from a knot. The combinations of techniques and materials that can be used are almost endless.

RECESSED

Illus. 198. Recessing is also achieved by bevel sawing. Note once more that there is no saw kerf space.

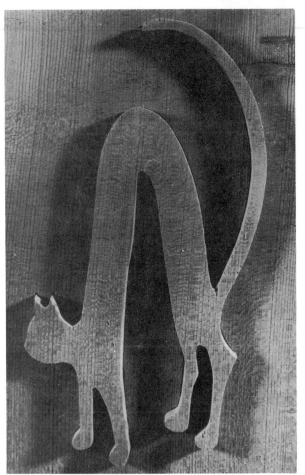

Illus. 199. A look at the rear back-side of a recessed object. This extra material can be worked flush to the back with a belt sander or by hand with a plane.

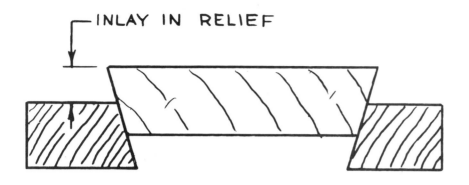

INLAY IN RELIEF

Illus. 200. Using a contrasting material for inlay relief.

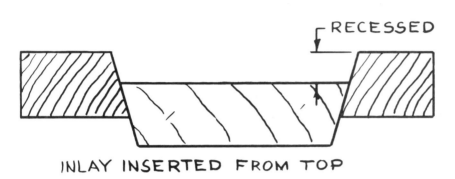

RECESSED

INLAY INSERTED FROM TOP

Illus. 201. Using contrasting material for recessed inlay.

PATTERN SECTION

11

SCROLL SAW PATTERNS

One of the problems common to all scroll-saw users is the difficulty of finding good, inexpensive, and easy-to-copy project patterns.

This selection of over 250 designs includes ideas for making household accessories such as wall plaques, pegboards, candle holders, and ornaments. Also included are many of the currently popular "country cutouts," puzzles, and projects incorporating the always delightful heart design. (Someone once told us, "If you want it to sell, put a heart on it." That bit of advice has proven to be true.)

There are many great projects in this selection that are easy for the beginner to make successfully. There are also a good number of somewhat-more-complex patterns intended for the experienced craftsperson and hobbyist. Many of the basic patterns are ideal for those individuals who enjoy woodburning (Illus. 202), painting (Illus. 203), stencilling, applying decals, and/or adding other individual touches. These decorative accents create beautiful household accessories and make great gifts. (Incidentally, a soft-tip marker [Illus. 204] can sometimes be used to color wood cutouts, but remember, it has a tendency to bleed on some softwoods.) The

different ways of implementing these patterns into completed projects are limited only by the imagination.

A scroll saw is the only tool needed to complete most of the projects. However, some also require the use of a hand or electric drill. It should also be noted that many of the designs and patterns here can also be cut out with a band saw.

Sears has two wood sign layout kits. These will be useful for making wooden signs, nameplates, and house numbers. If you are interested in making wood signs, one book worth reading is *Making Wood Signs*, available at Sears through either retail sales or its catalog.

The advanced craftsperson will find some patterns for fretwork shelves, shelf brackets, picture frames, and compound sawing projects. There is also an abundance of ideas for fancy scroll-saw inlays, segmented pictures, and marquetry designs. Many patterns can be used simply as a starting point for the creative woodworker. If, for example, you need a leaf design for an inlaid jewelry box, you'll find some design ideas here, but you can expand on these designs.

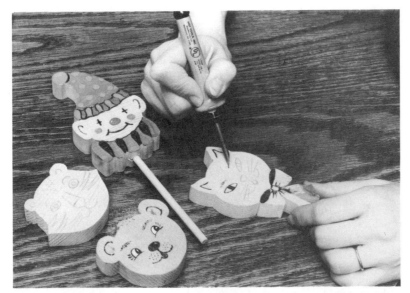

Illus. 202. Some details can be outlined with a woodburning tool.

Illus. 203. You can add a touch of color with craft paint.

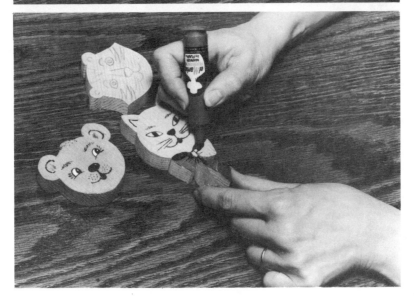

Illus. 204. Soft-tip markers can be used to color areas outlined with a woodburning tool.

Creatures of the Deep

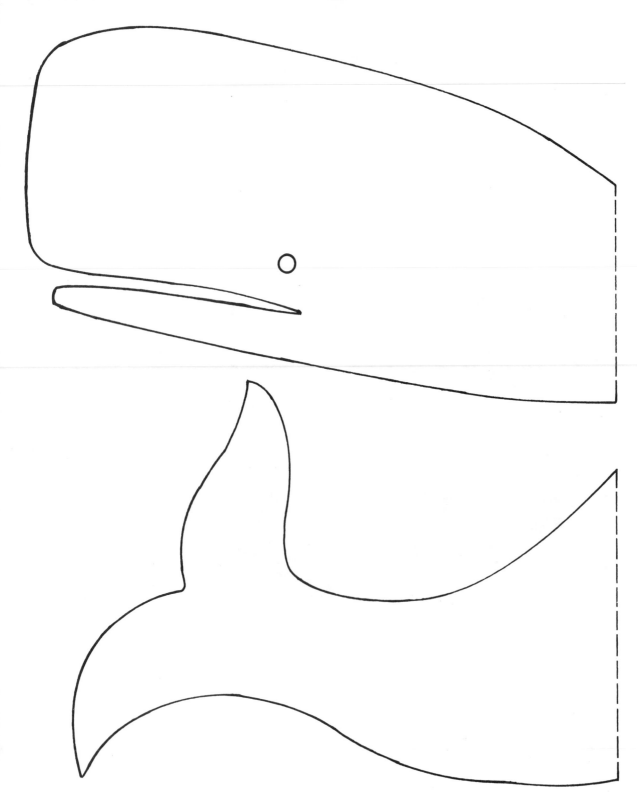

Illus. 205.

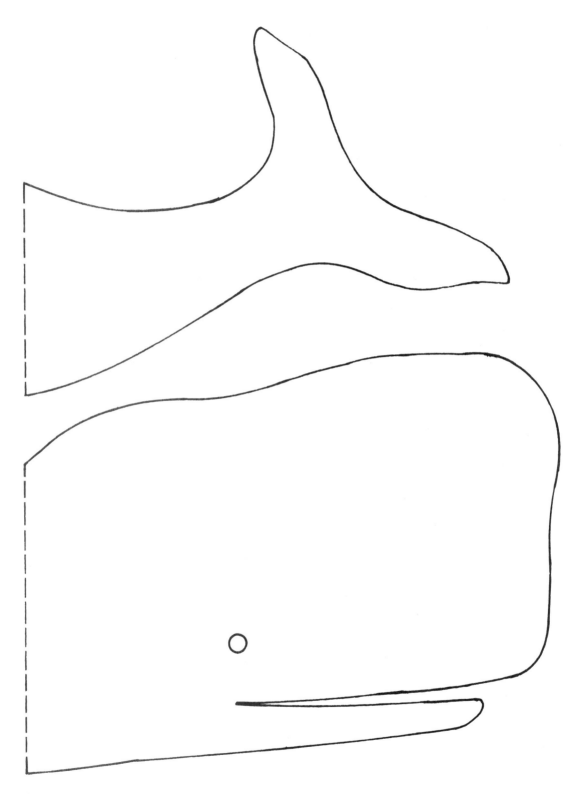

Illus. 205 continued.

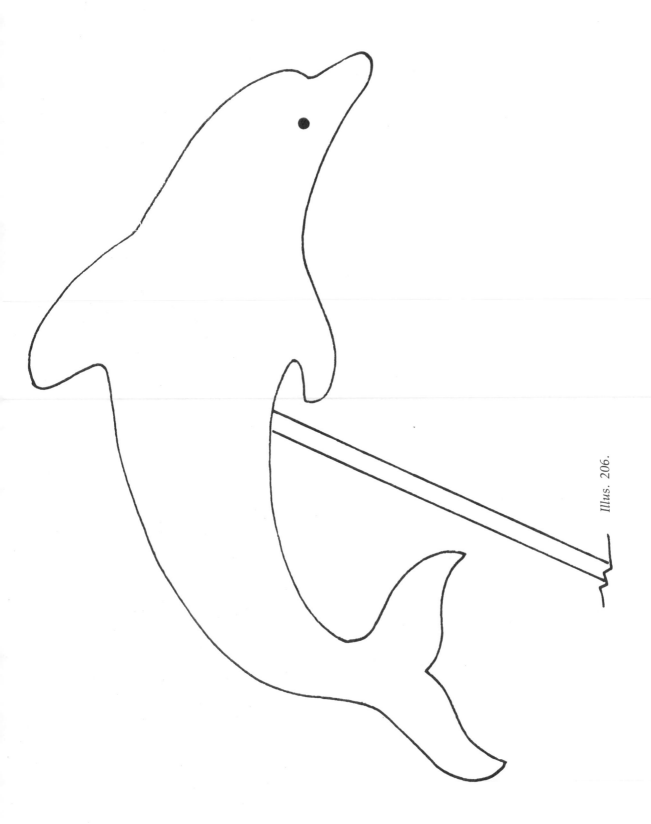

Illus. 206.

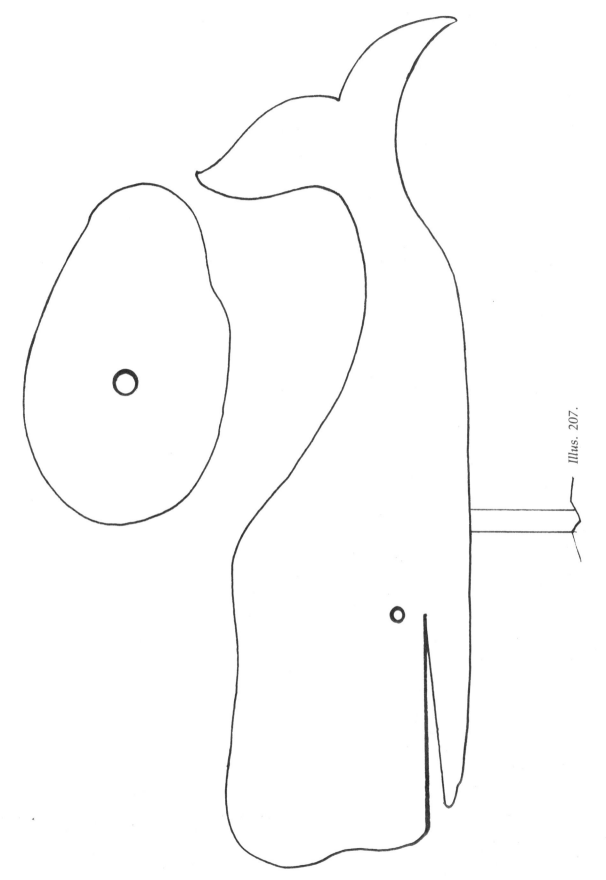

Illus. 207.

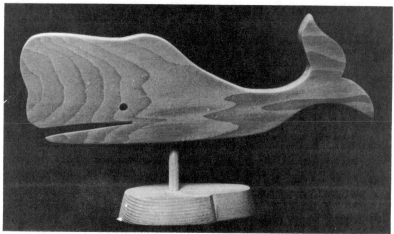

Illus. 208. Photo of whale shown on page 105.

Birds

Illus. 209.

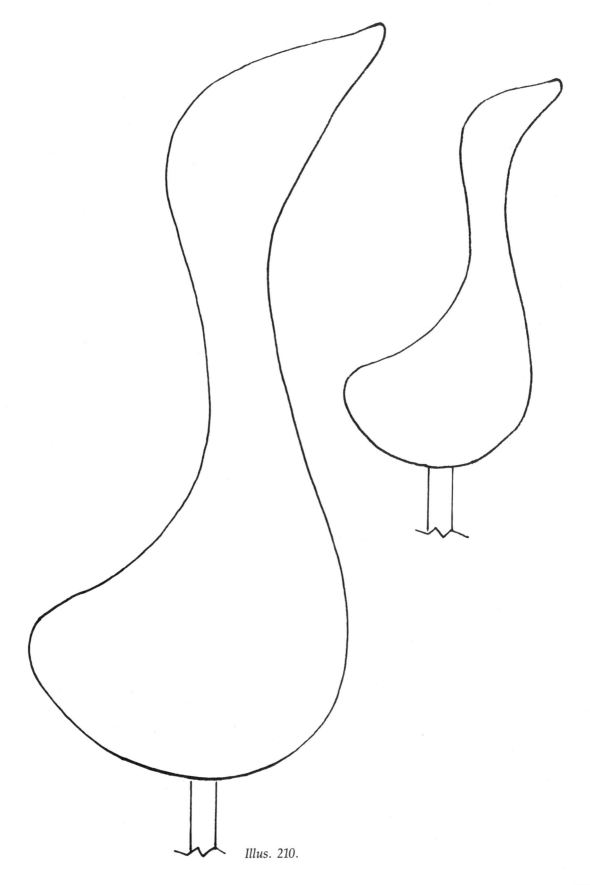

Illus. 210.

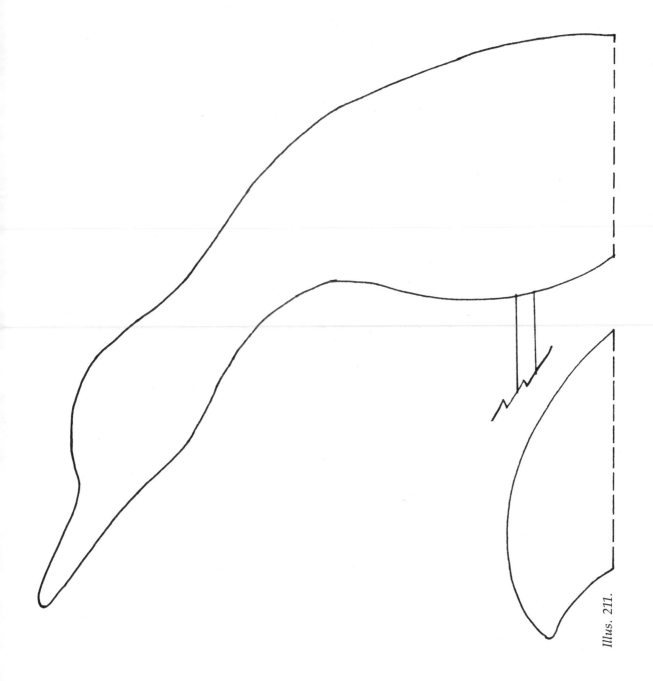

Illus. 211.

108

Illus. 211 continued.

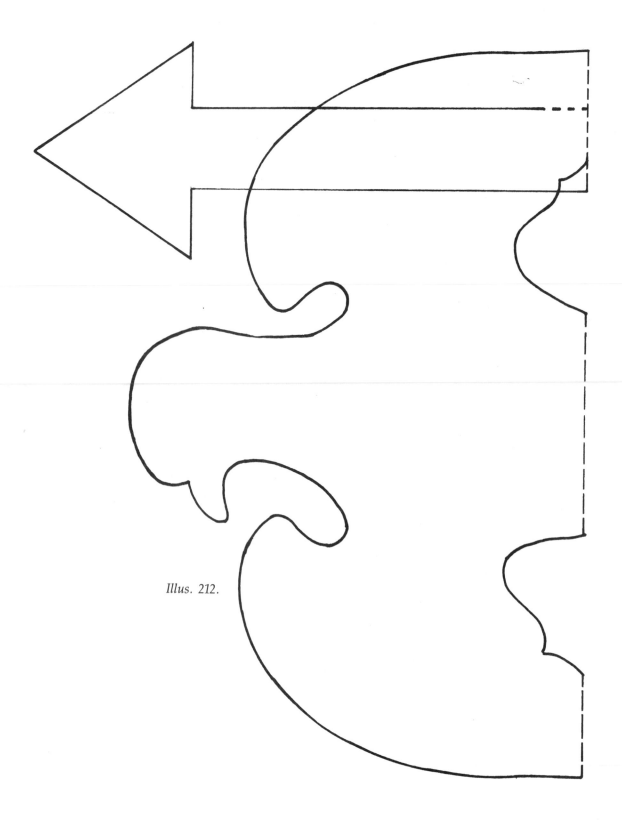

Illus. 212.

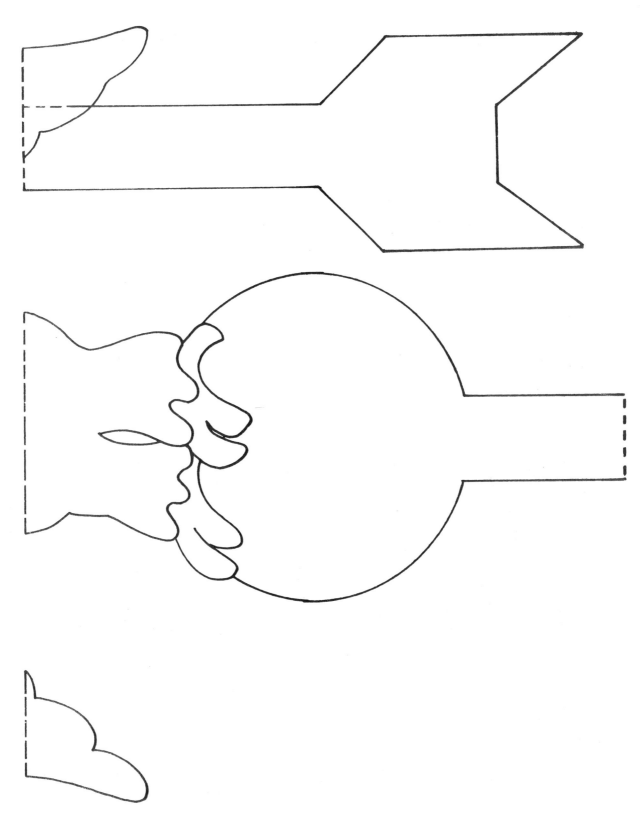

Illus. 212 continued.

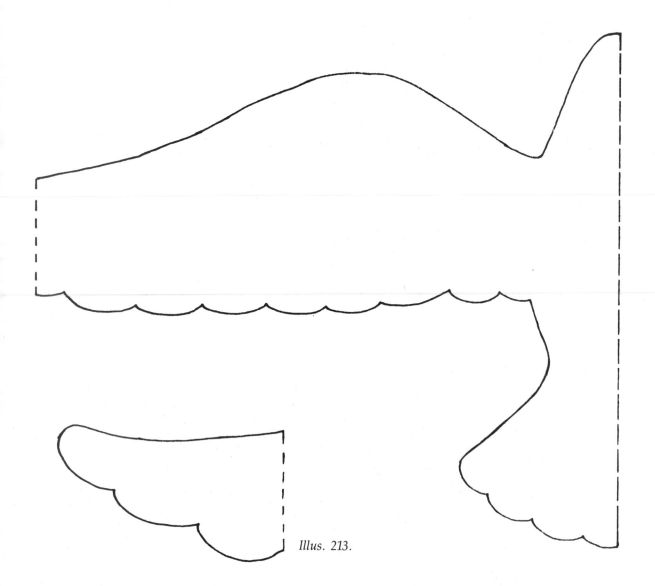

Illus. 213.

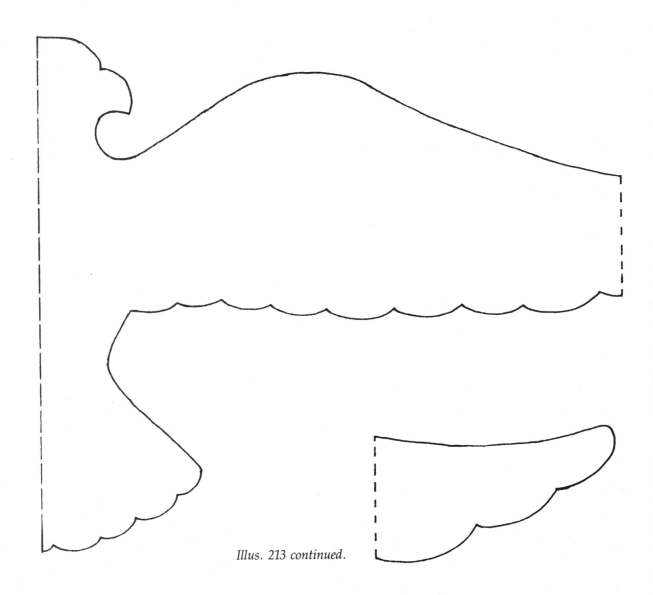

Illus. 213 continued.

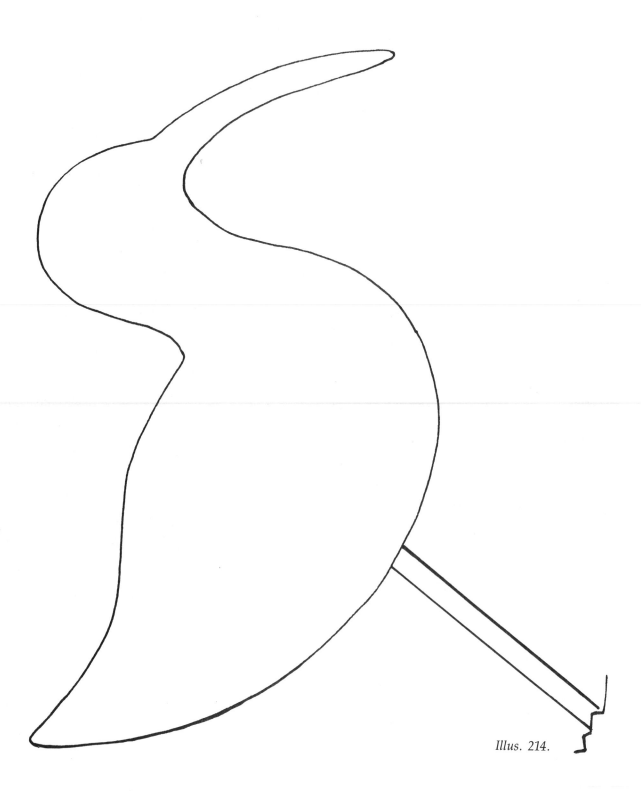

Illus. 214.

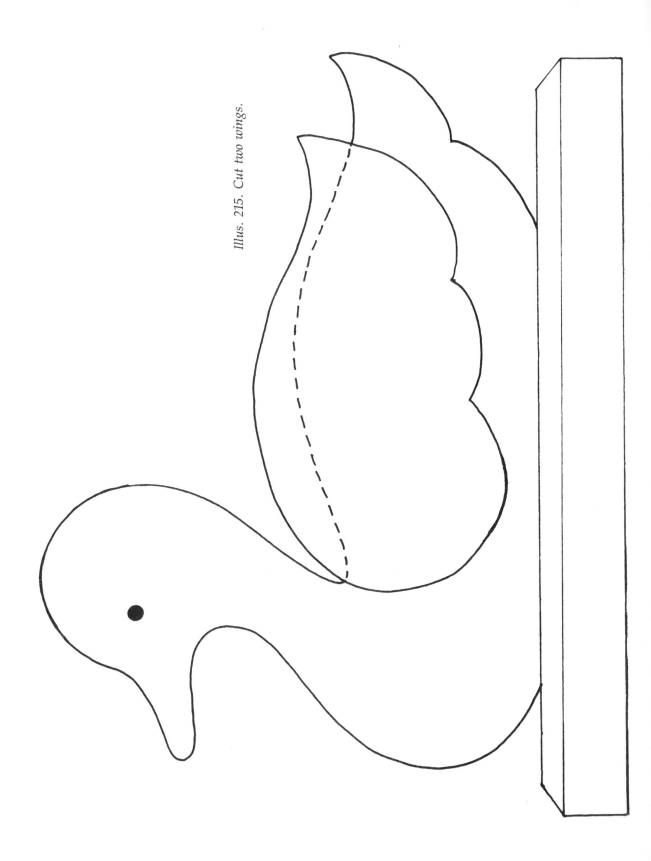

Illus. 215. Cut two wings.

115

Illus. 216.

Illus. 217. Cut two wings.

Illus. 218.

Illus. 219.

Illus. 220.

Illus. 221.

Illus. 222.

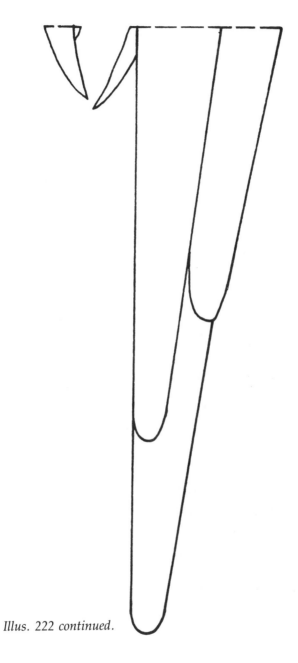

Illus. 222 continued.

Illus. 223.

Illus. 224.

Illus. 225.

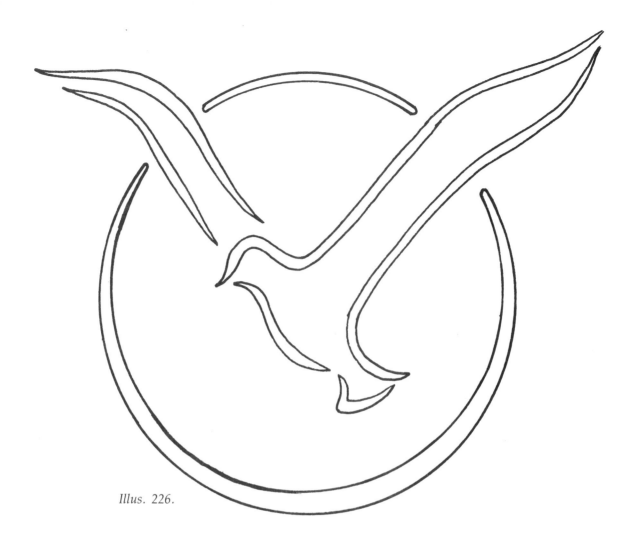

Illus. 226.

Illus. 227. Gull design that has been cut through. Such designs can be used for signboards or clockfaces.

Key Racks

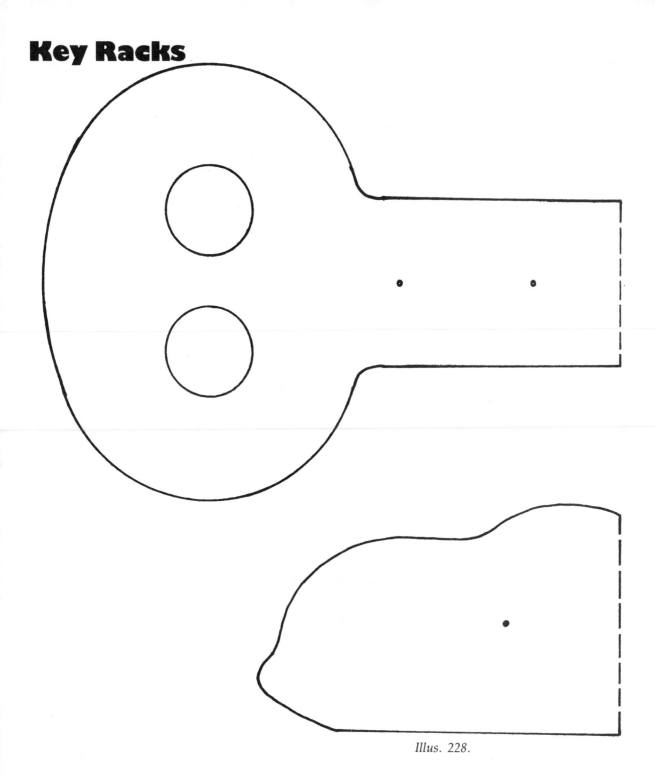

Illus. 228.

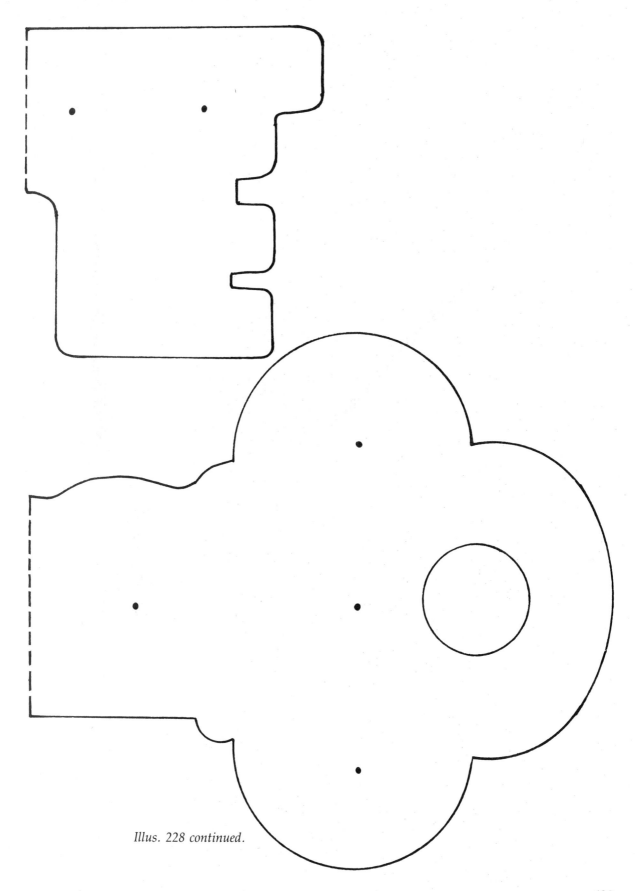

Illus. 228 continued.

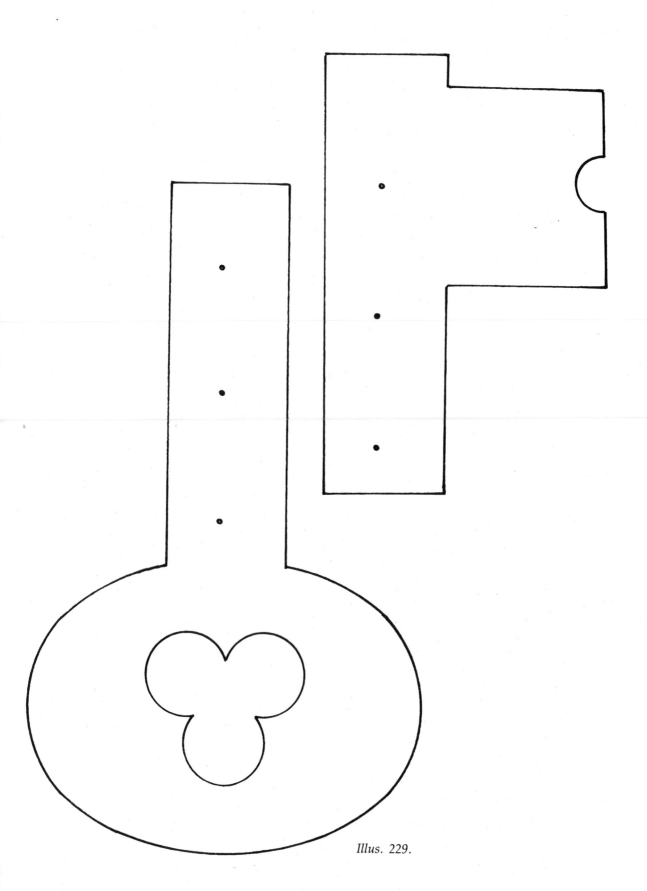

Illus. 229.

Interlocking Trees/Corner Shelves

Illus. 230. Interlocking trees cut from ¼-inch plywood.

Illus. 231. Corner shelf with ¼-inch-thick sides; the shelf is ⅜ inch thick.

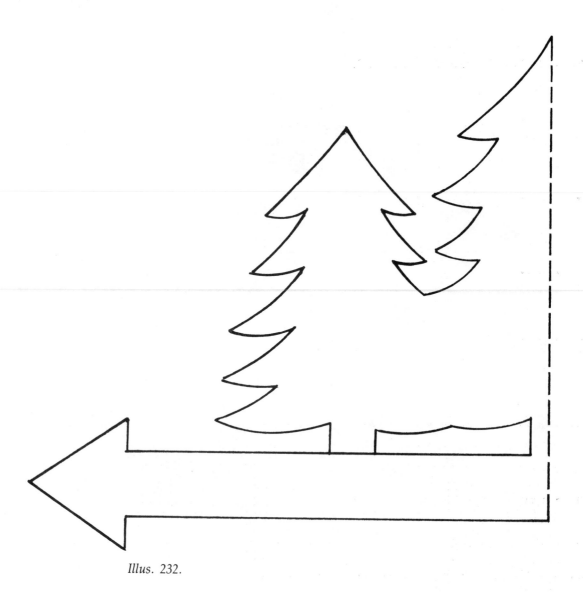

Illus. 232.

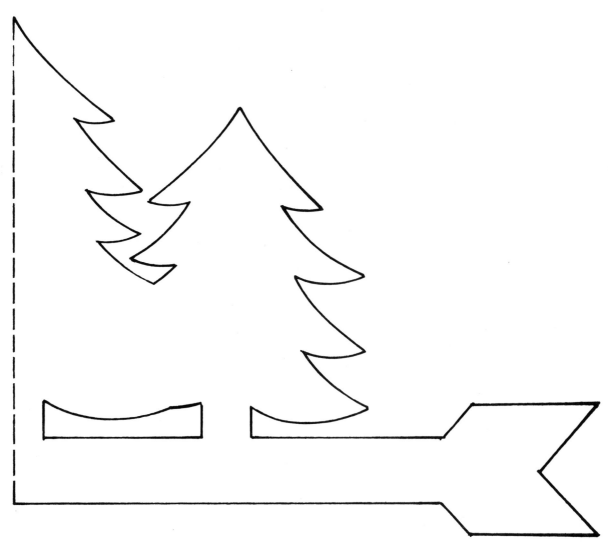

Illus. 232 continued.

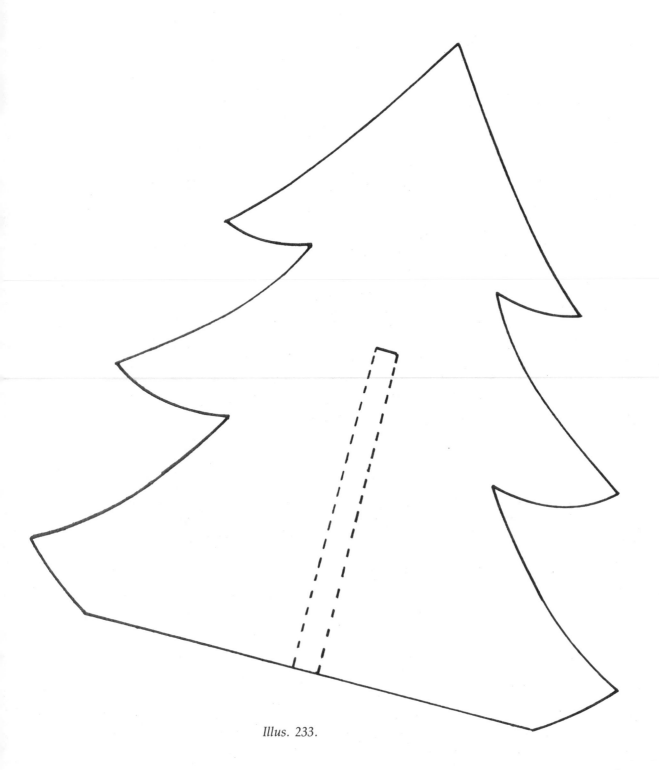

Illus. 233.

Illus. 234.

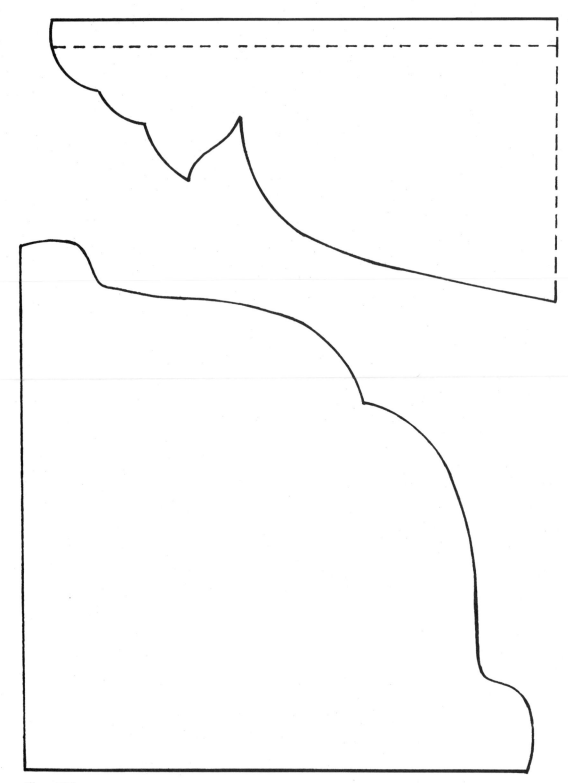

Illus. 235.

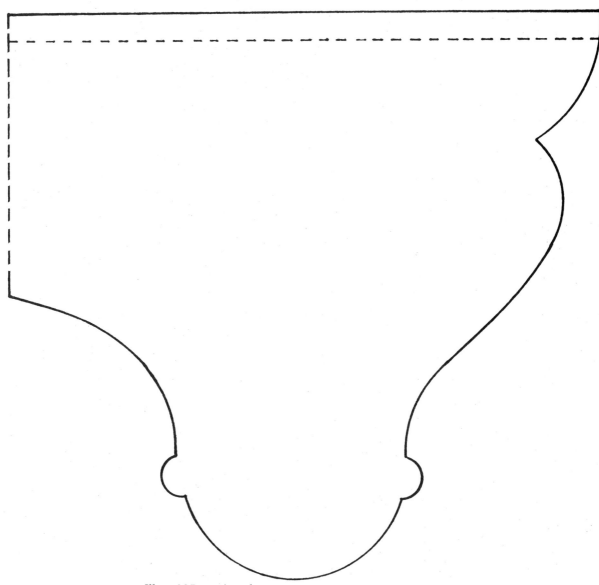

Illus. 235 continued.

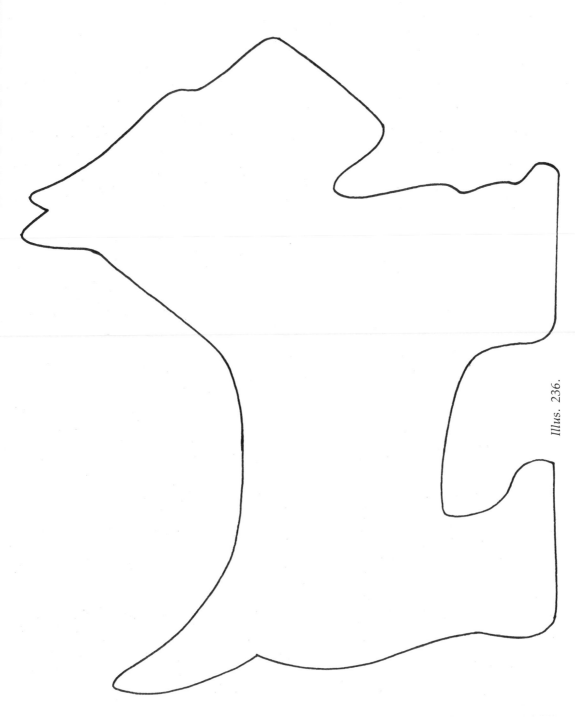

Illus. 236.

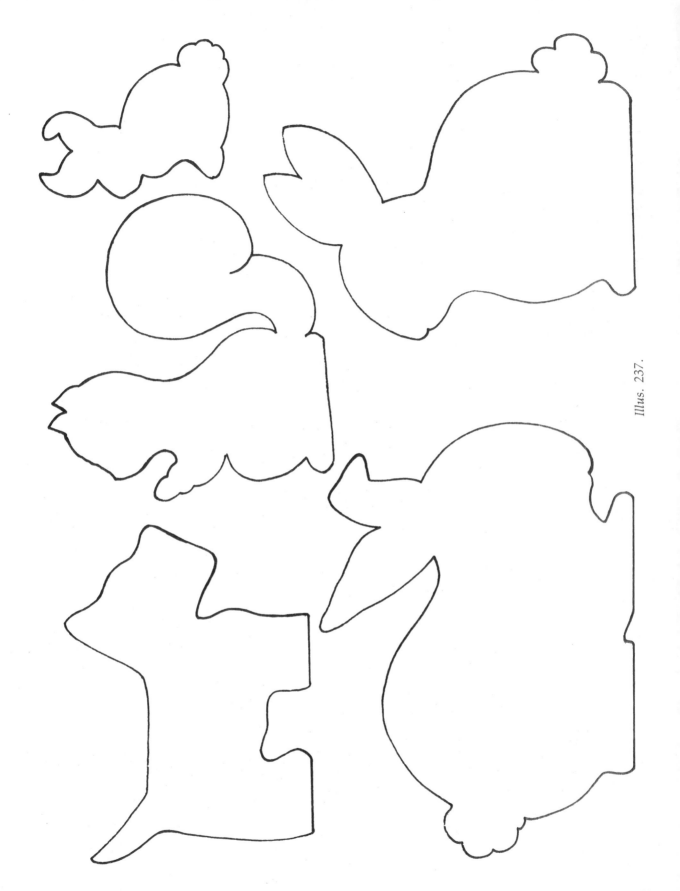

Illus. 238. Goldilocks and the Three Bears. A photo appears on the following page.

Illus. 239. Goldilocks and the Three Bears.

Mini-Animal Cutouts

Illus. 240. Mini-animal cutouts.

Belt Hook Designs

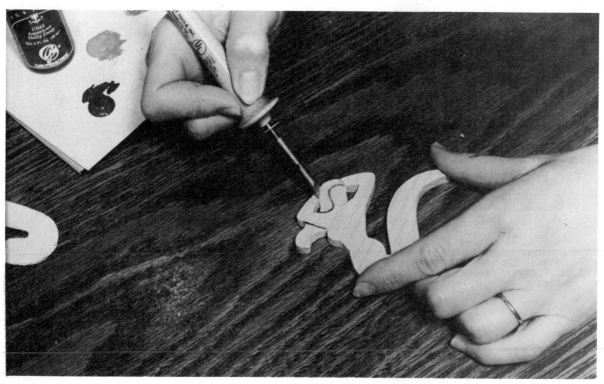

Illus. 243. Woodburning lines on a mermaid belt hook.

Illus. 244. A variety of belt hook designs cut from ¼- to ⅜-inch stock.

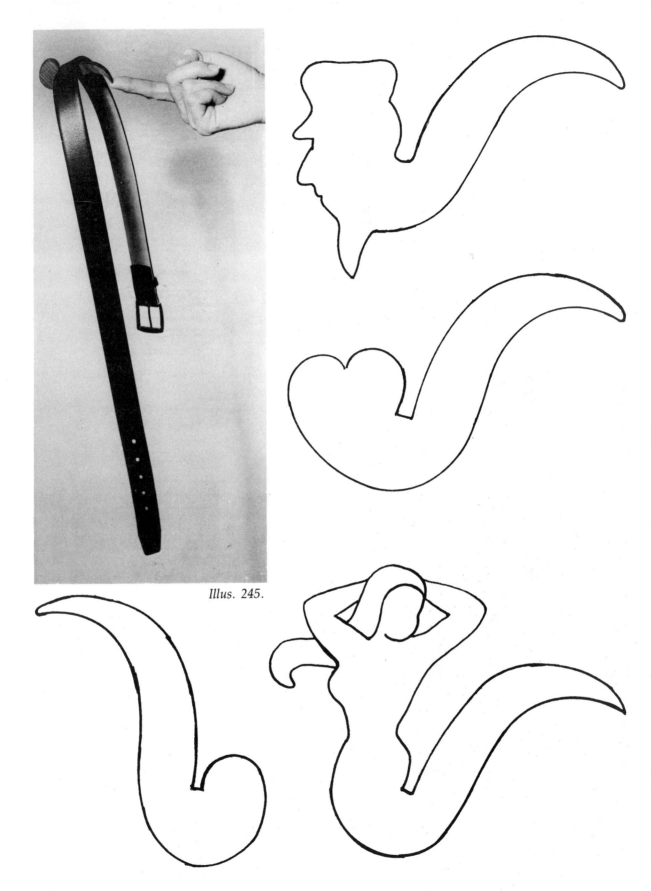

Illus. 245.

Illus. 247. *Cat and flowers.*

Illus. 248.

146

Dimensional Animal Cutouts

Illus. 249.

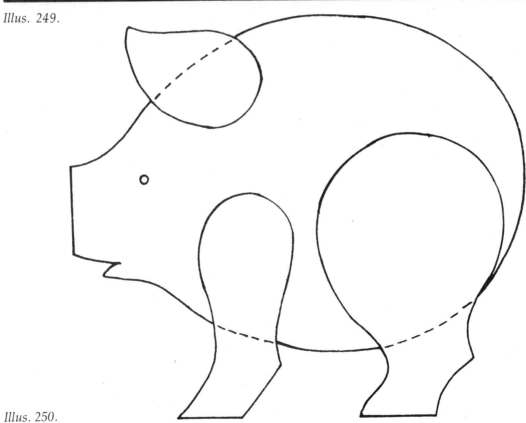

Illus. 250.

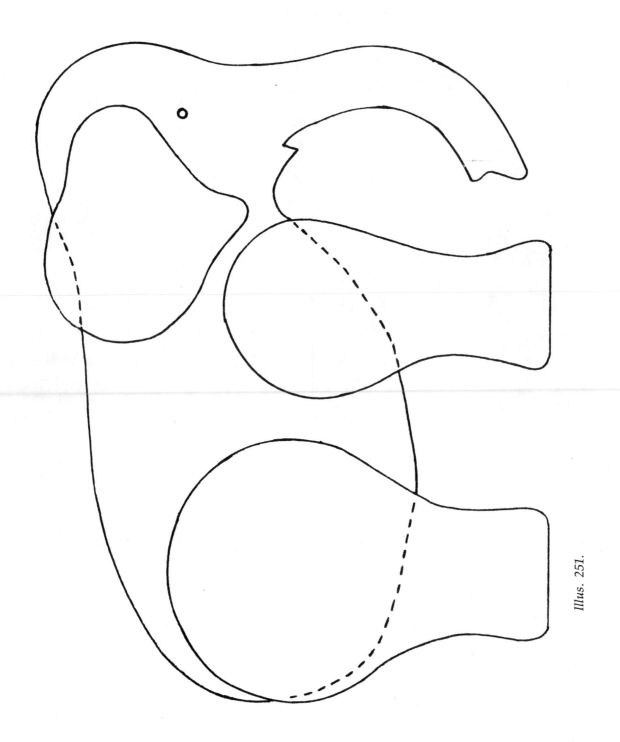

Illus. 251.

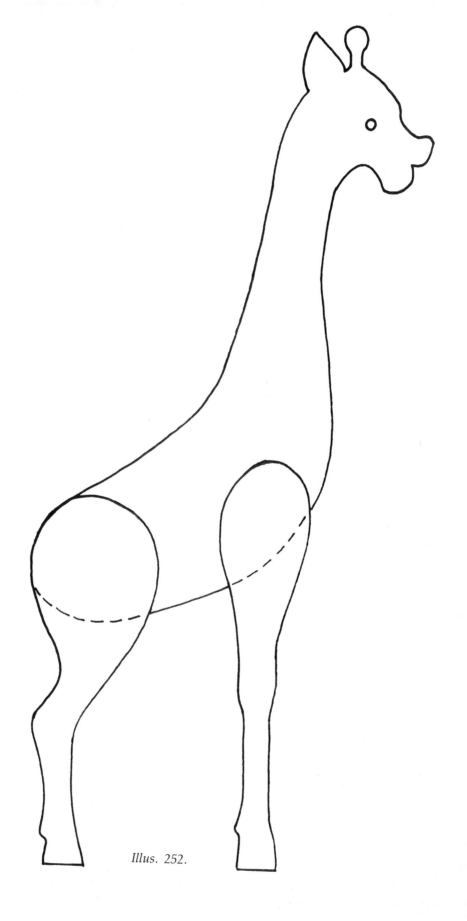

Illus. 252.

Illus. 253.

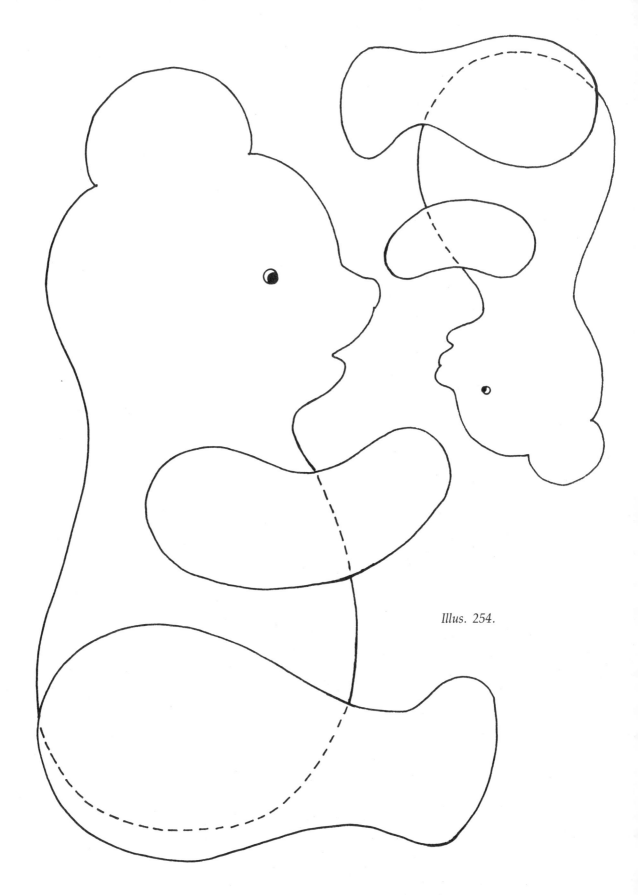

Illus. 254.

Refrigerator Magnets/ "Pets on a Stick"

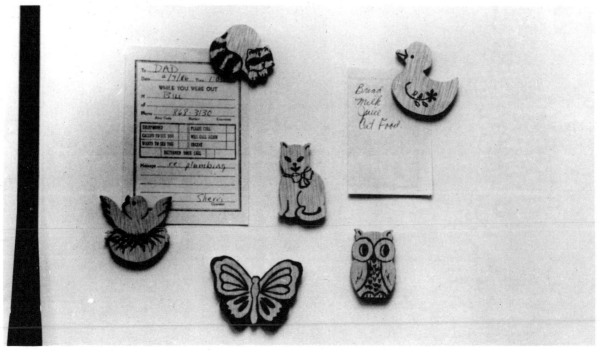

Illus. 255. The refrigerator magnets are cut from ¼-inch stock; epoxy is put on purchased magnets. Patterns for refrigerator magnets can be found on pages 153 and 154.

Illus. 256. "Pets on a Stick." Patterns for the "Pets" can be found on page 155.

Illus. 257.

Illus. 259.

Illus. 260.

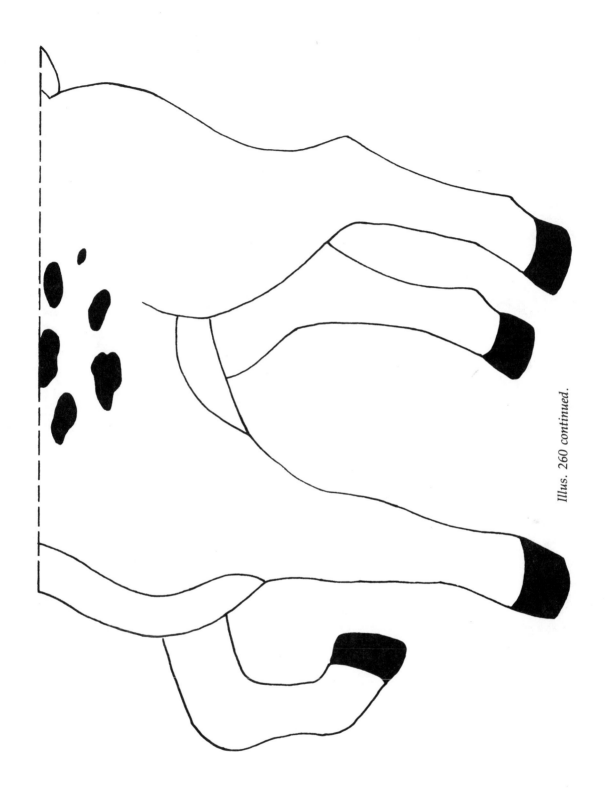

Illus. 260 continued.

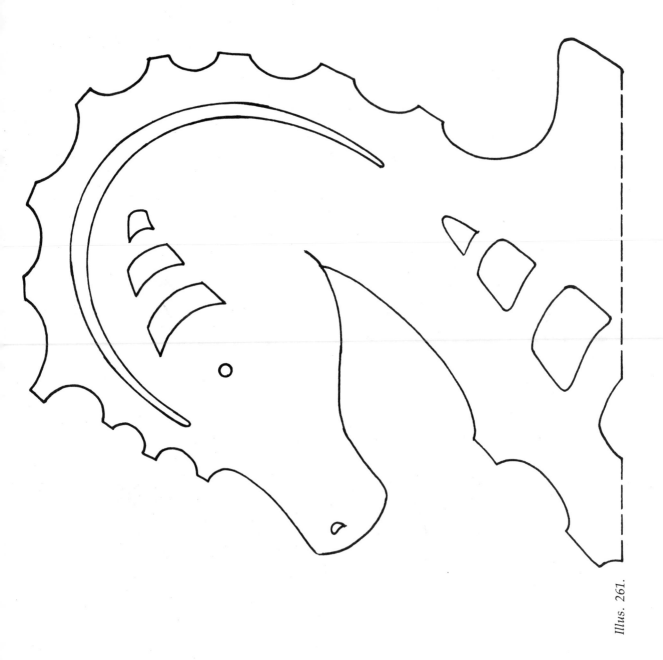

Illus. 261.

Illus. 261 continued.

Napkin Rings/Puzzles

Illus. 262. Napkin rings. Patterns can be found on pages 161 and 162.

Illus. 263. Puzzles. Above: Cutout from thick stock. Below: Inlay puzzle cut from ¼-inch plywood with ¼-inch plywood backing. Patterns can be found on pages 163–175.

Illus. 266.

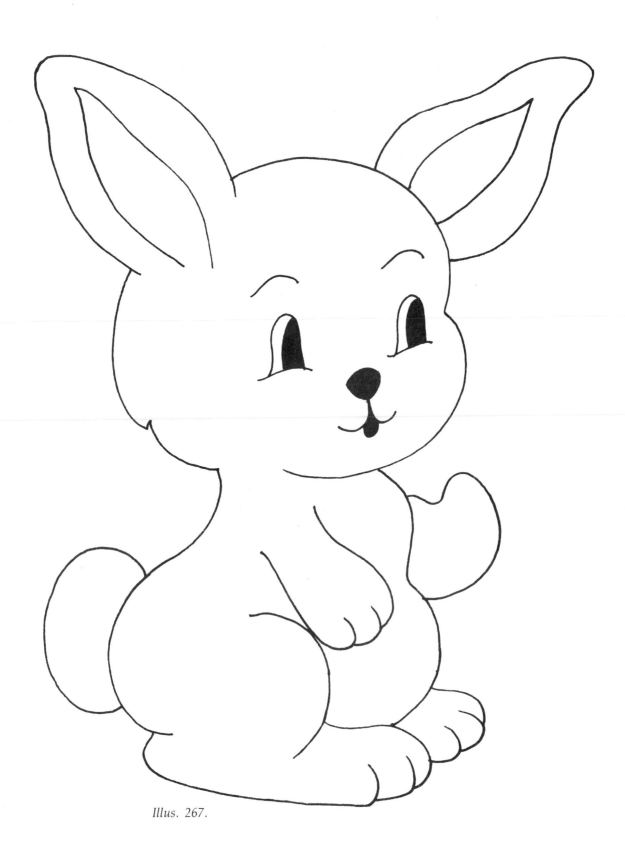

Illus. 267.

Illus. 268.

Illus. 269.

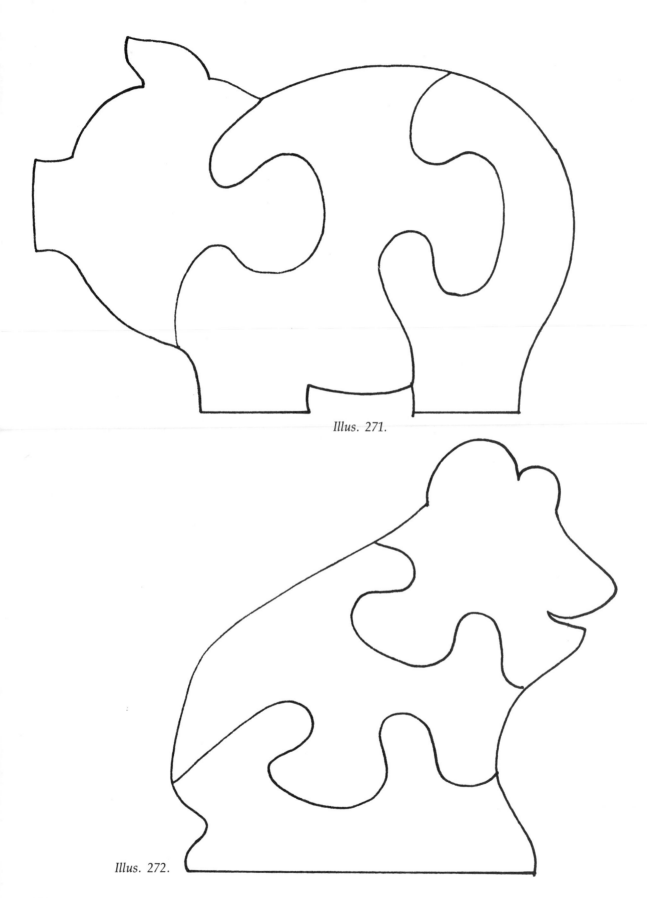

Illus. 271.

Illus. 272.

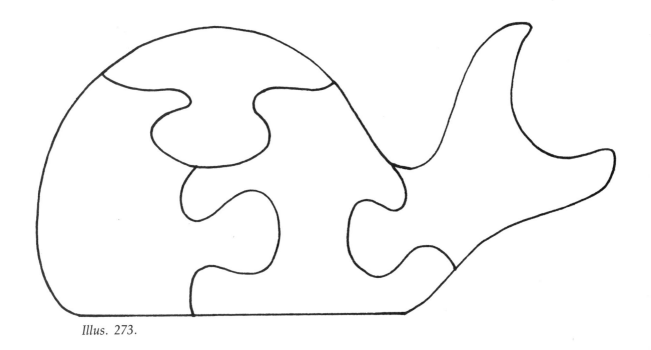

Illus. 273.

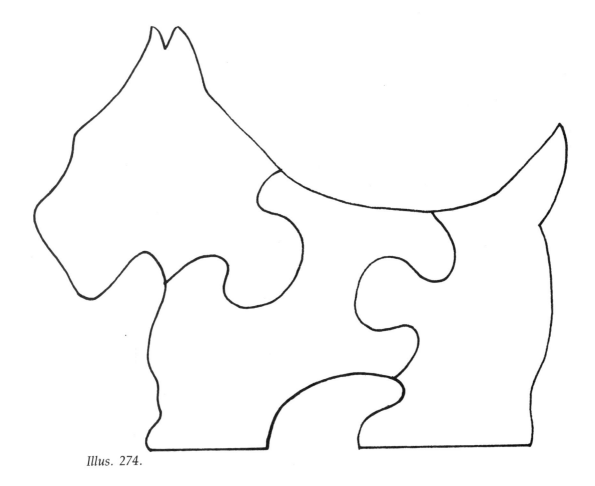

Illus. 274.

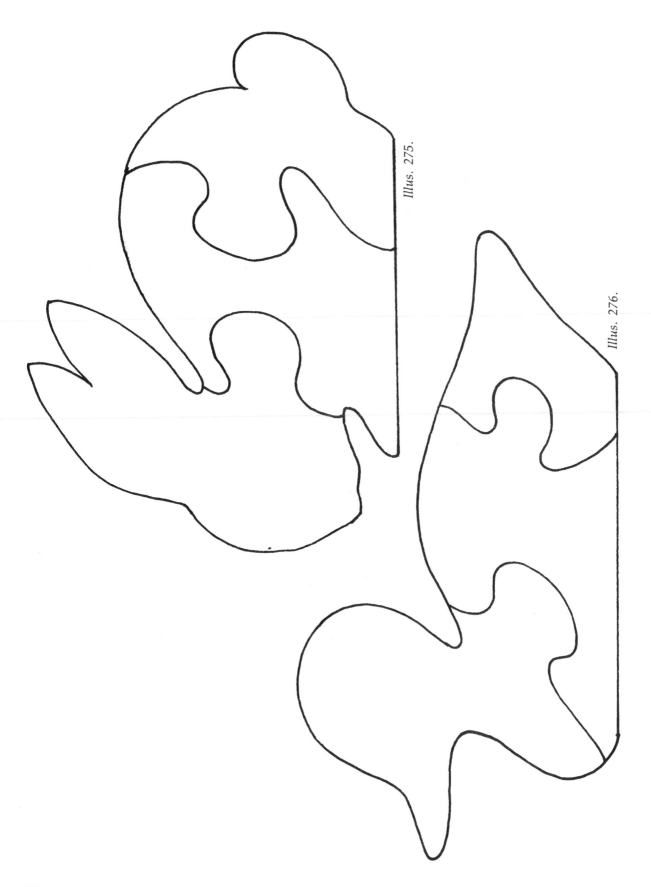

Illus. 275.

Illus. 276.

Illus. 278.

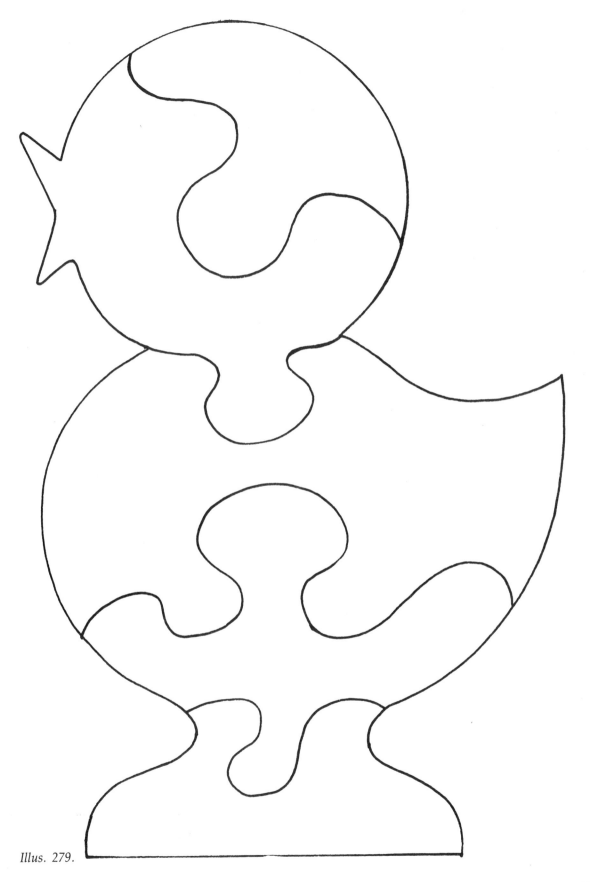

Illus. 279.

Illus. 280.

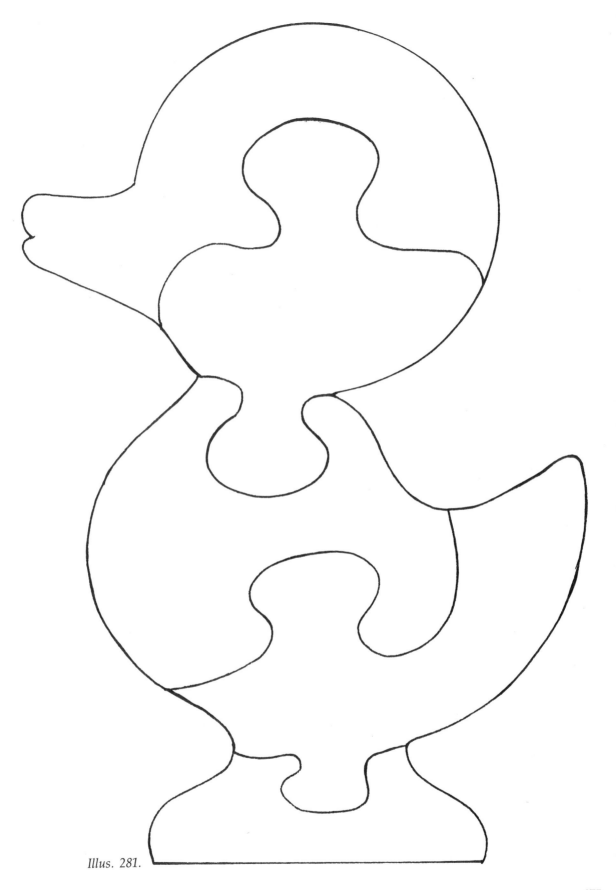

Illus. 281.

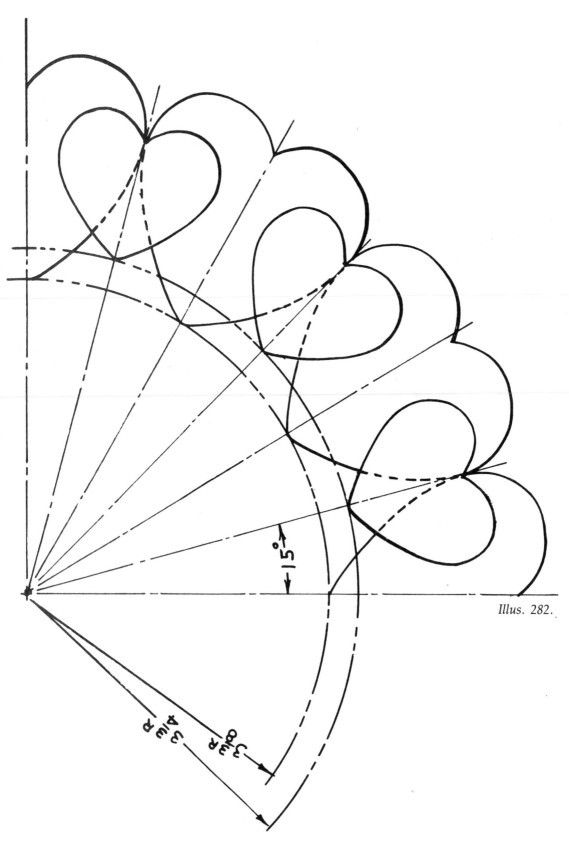

Illus. 282.

15°

3 R

3 4 R

3 R 8

Illus. 283. Heart wreath and candle holders.

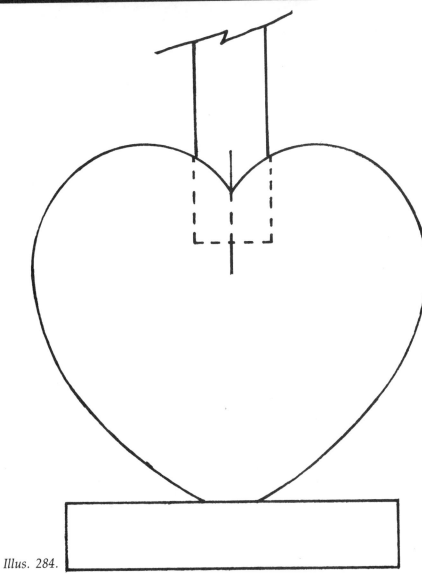

Illus. 284.

Jewelry/Ornaments

Illus. 285. *These items of jewelry were made from brass and ⅛-inch-thick exotic hardwoods. The key chains were made from ¼-inch plywood.*

Illus. 286. *Ornaments made from ¼-inch material.*

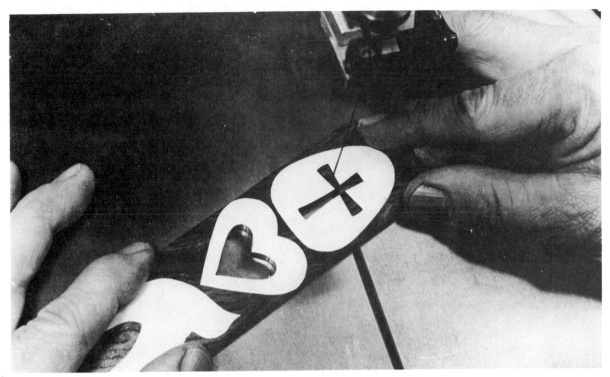

Illus. 287. Sawing out jewelry. Paper patterns are glued to the work with rubber cement.

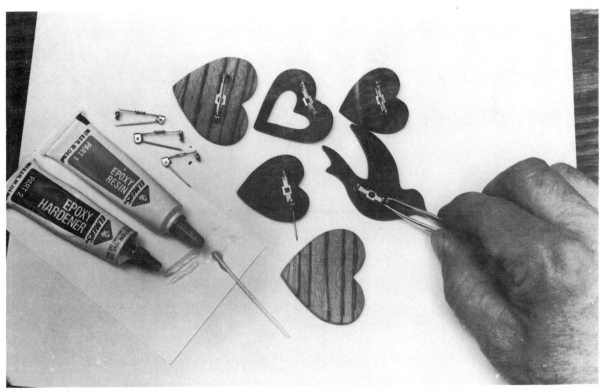

Illus. 288. Use epoxy to bond findings to the cutouts.

Illus. 289.

Illus. 290.

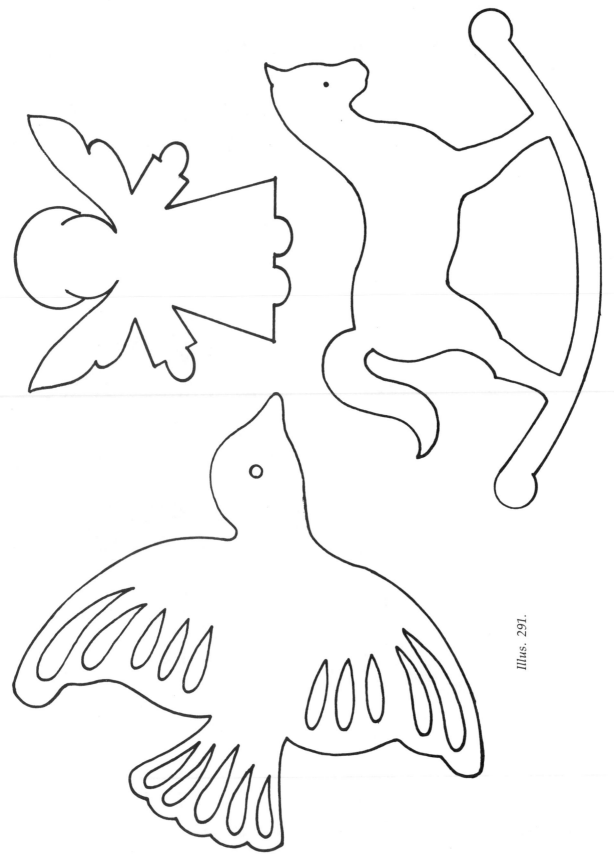

Illus. 291.

184

Candle Holders/Pegboards/Brackets

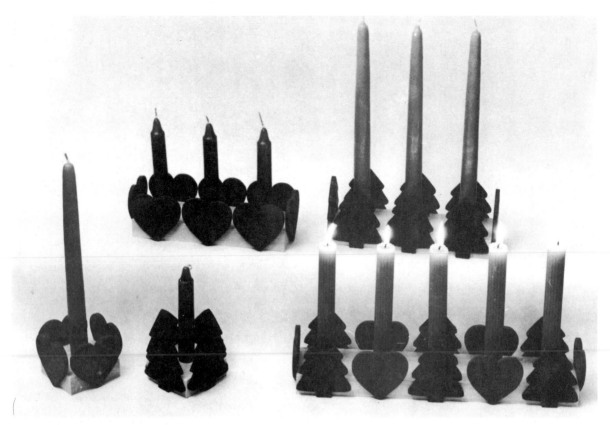

Illus. 297. Candle holders. Use ¼-inch material for cutouts. Patterns can be found on pages 190 and 191.

Illus. 298. Pegboards.

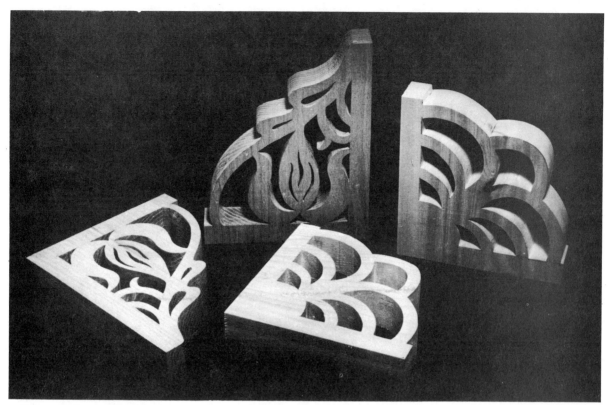

Illus. 299. Corner brackets.

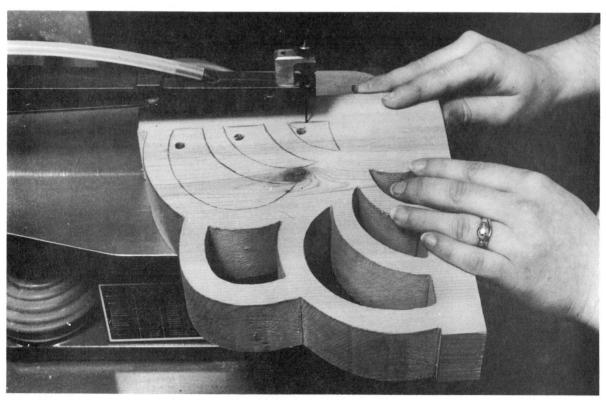

Illus. 300. Sawing a corner bracket from 1¾-inch-thick stock.

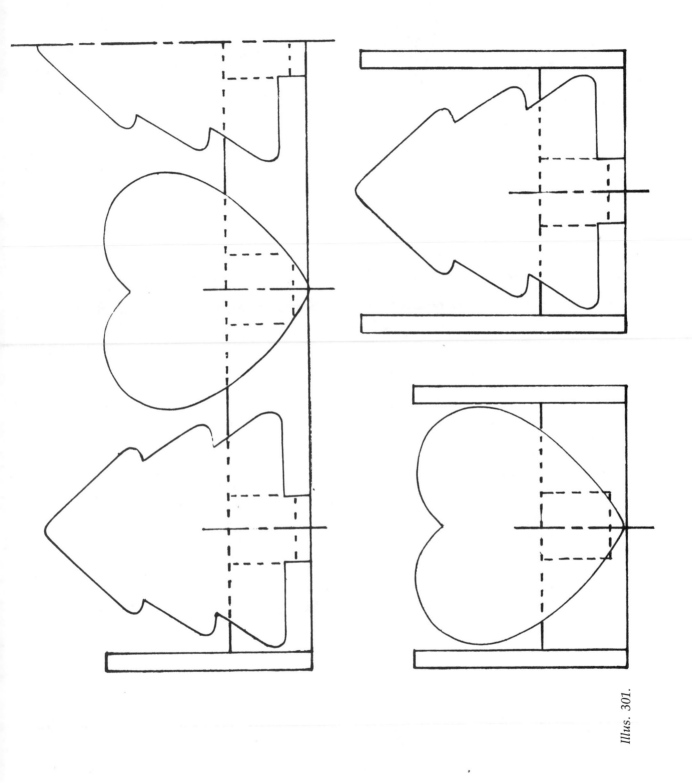

Illus. 301.

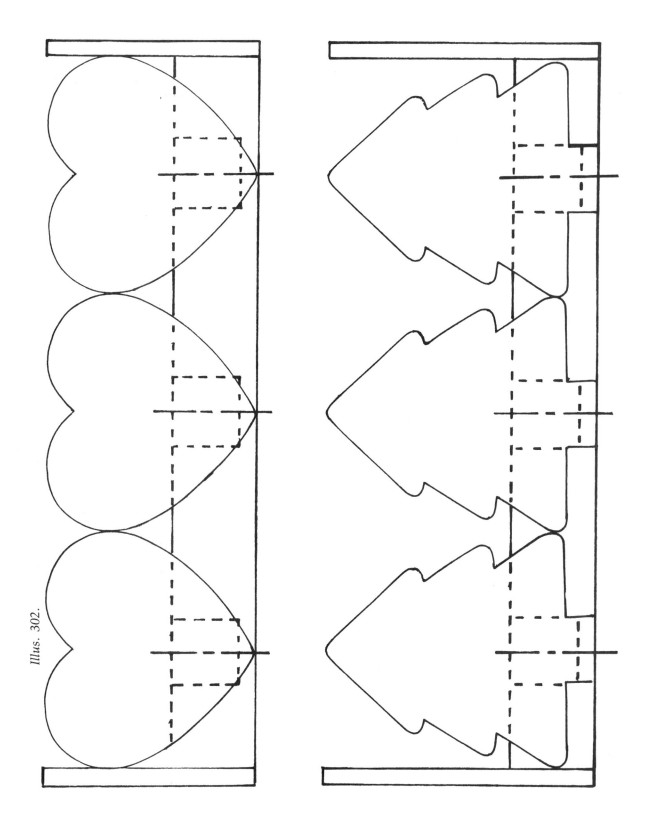

Illus. 302.

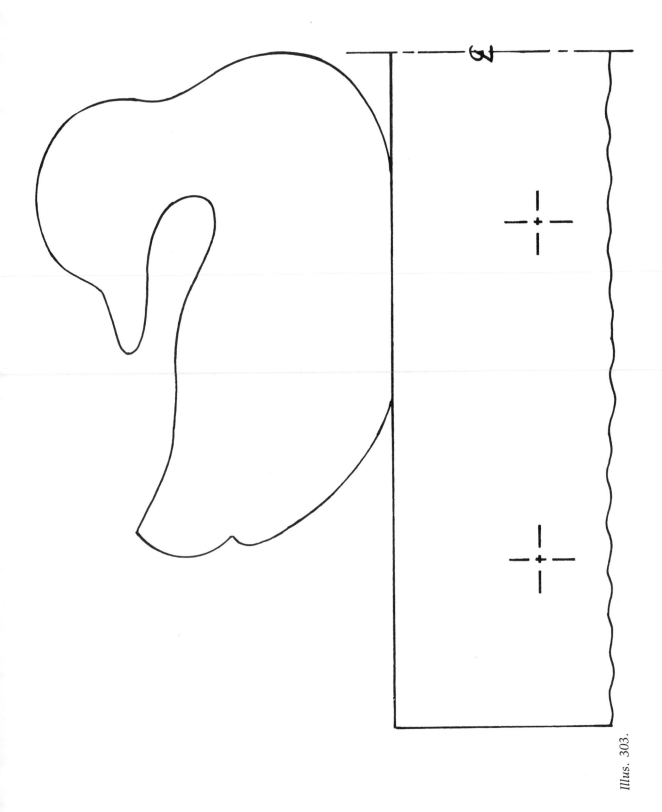

Illus. 303.

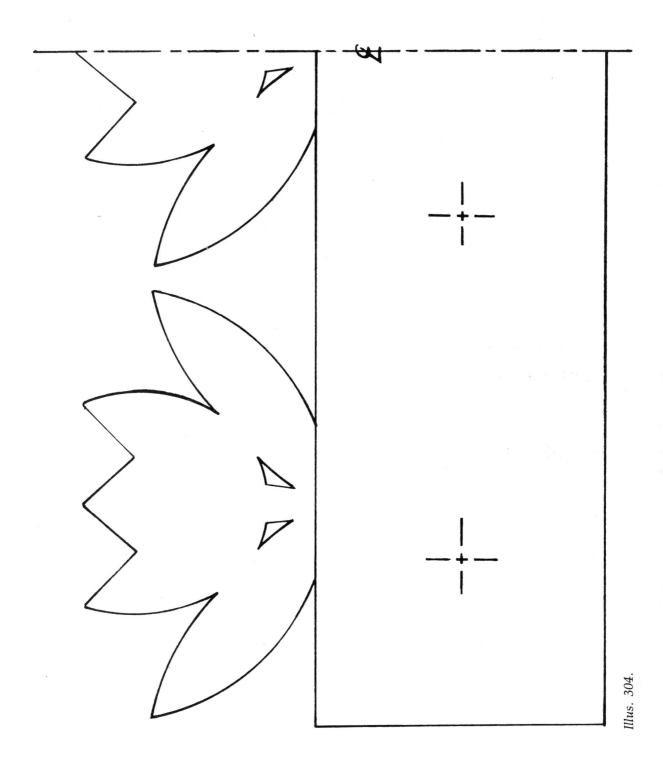

Illus. 304.

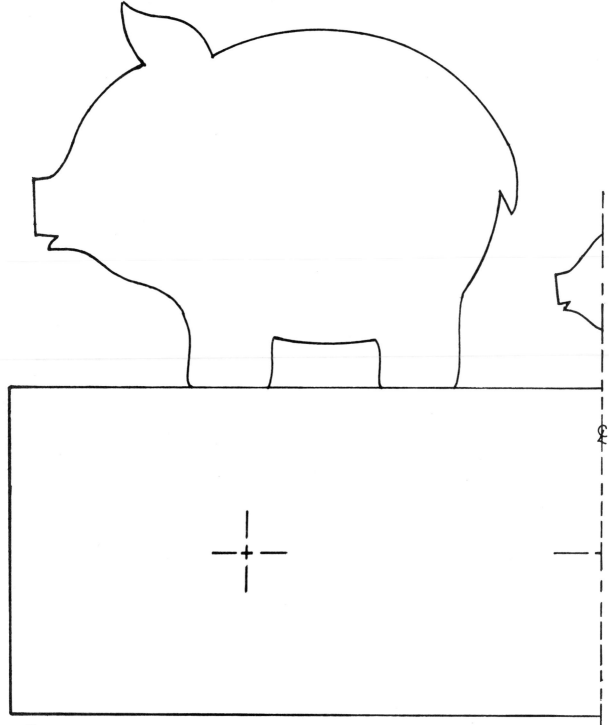

Illus. 305.

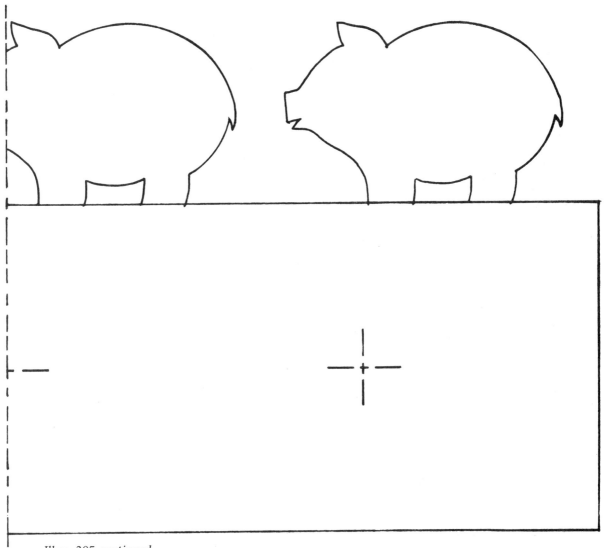

Illus. 305 continued.

Illus. 306.

ALIGN A's

A

ALIGN A's.

Illus. 306 continued.

Illus. 307.

Illus. 308.

Illus. 309.

Illus. 310.

200

Shelf

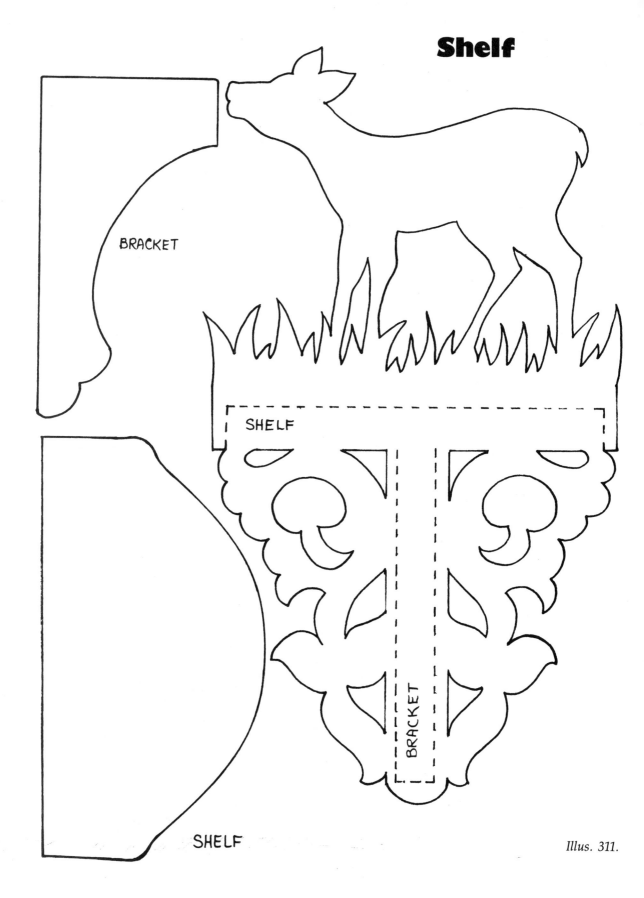

BRACKET

SHELF

BRACKET

SHELF

Illus. 311.

Illus. 313. Recessed design.

Illus. 312. Simple cutout.

Illus. 315. Simple silhouette sawn in a slab.

Illus. 314. Designs in relief.

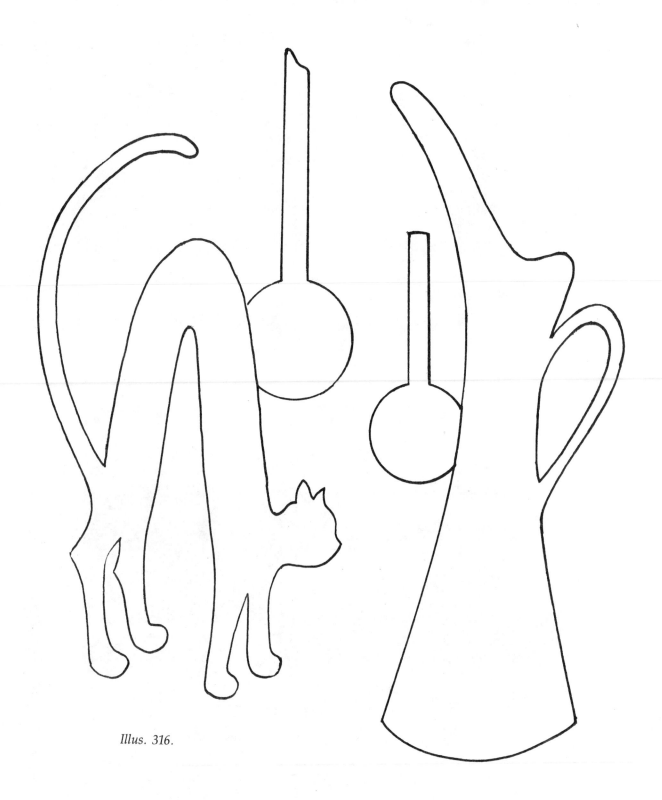

Illus. 316.

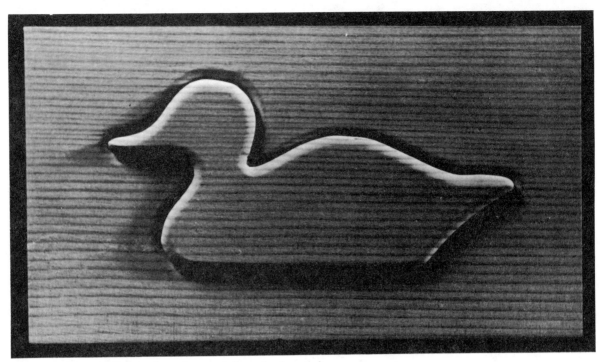

Illus. 317. Simple line work, cut, rounded, and reinserted.

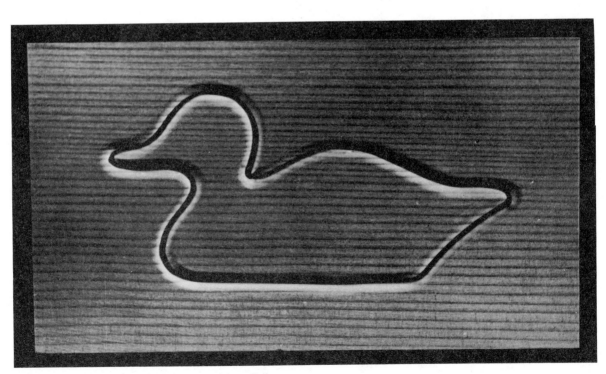

Illus. 318. The same idea, but inserted in relief.

Illus. 319.

Illus. 320.

Illus. 321.

Illus. 322.

Lamp Assembly

Illus. 323 and 324. Hanging hex lamps (above and below).

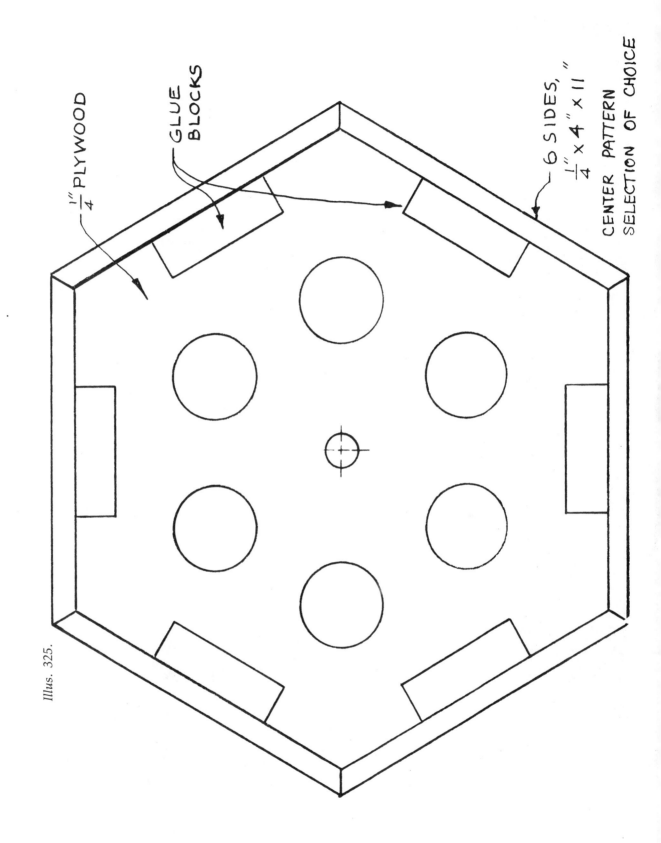

GLUE BLOCKS

$\frac{1}{4}$" PLYWOOD

6 SIDES, $\frac{1}{4}$" x **4**" x 11"

CENTER PATTERN
SELECTION OF CHOICE

Illus. 325.

211

Illus. 326.

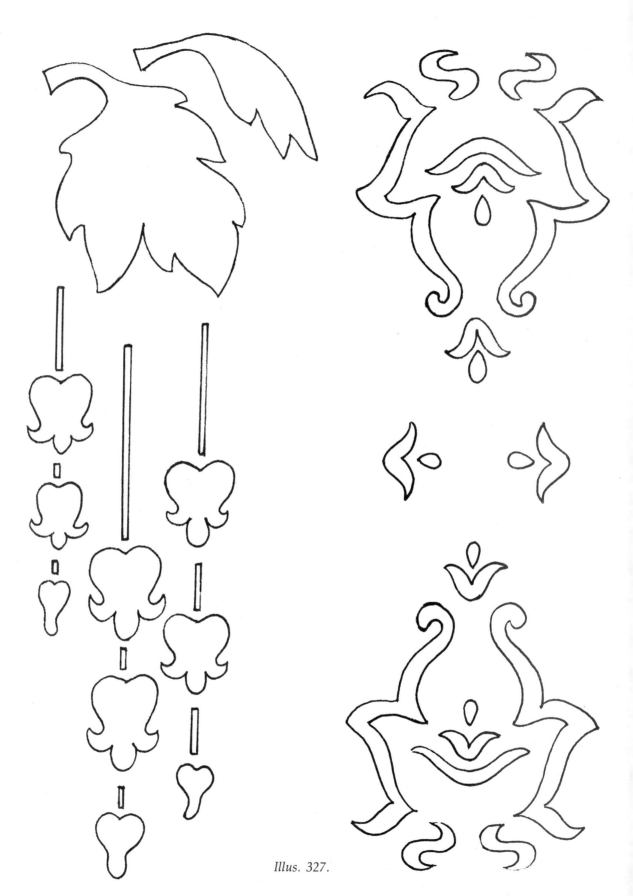

Illus. 327.

Illus. 328.

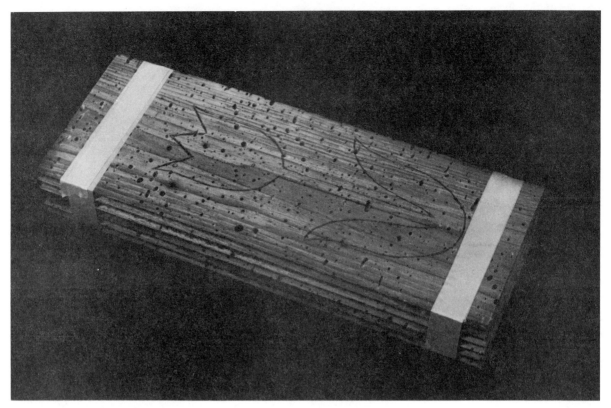

Illus. 329. With the pattern centered in sized stock with 60-degree edges, stack the boards together for multiple sawing.

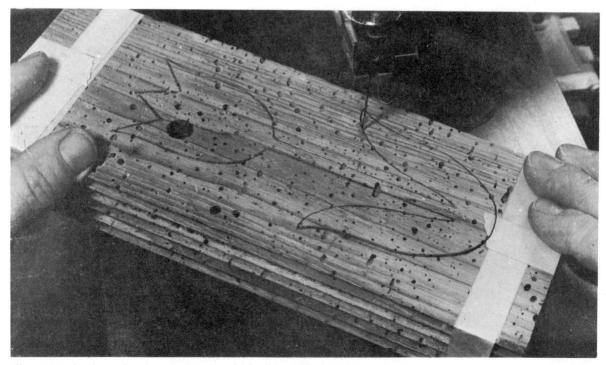

Illus. 330. Stack-sawing is a process in which all six sides are cut at one time.

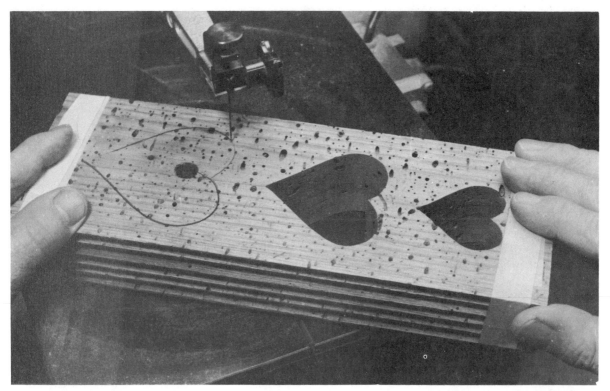

Illus. 331. Stack-sawing for another lamp.

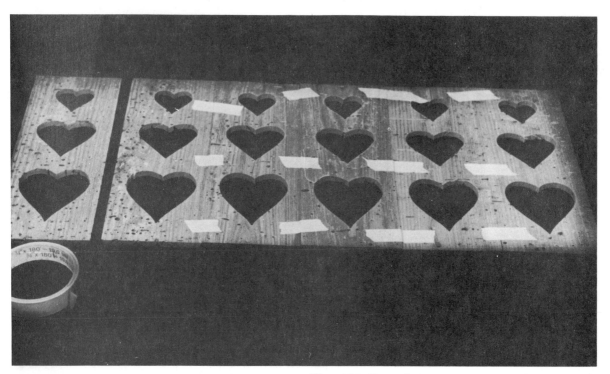

Illus. 332. Tape all six pieces together on the face side.

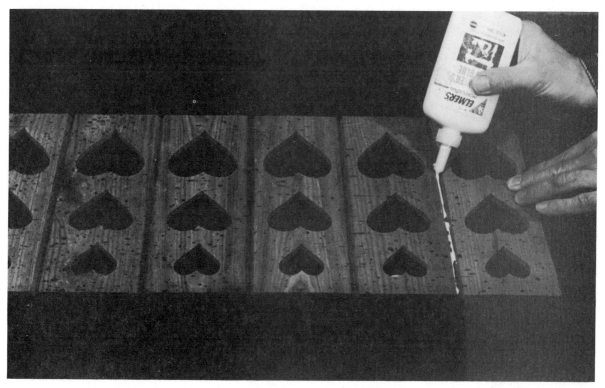

Illus. 333. Flip all taped pieces over and spread glue in the "V" openings.

Illus. 334. Pull the assembly together. The tape acts as a hinge and clamp.

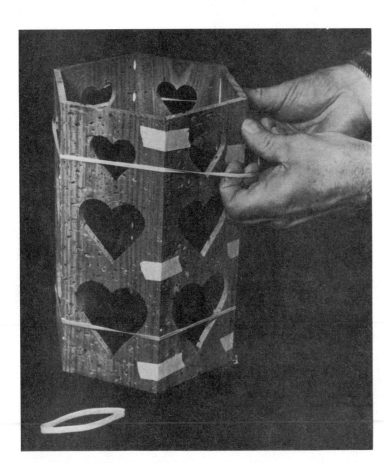

Illus. 335. A few heavy rubber
bands provide the clamping pressure.

Illus. 336. The hex top is secured with triangular glue blocks.

218

Compound Sawing

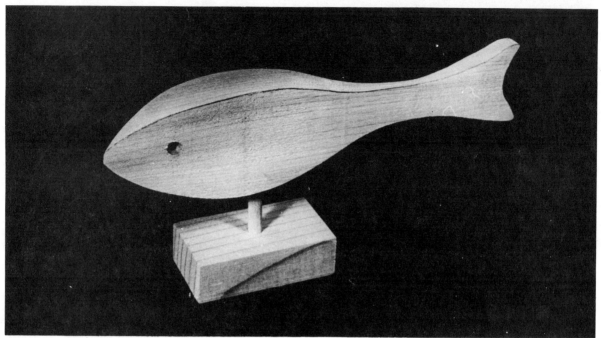

Illus. 337. Simple fish formed by compound sawing.

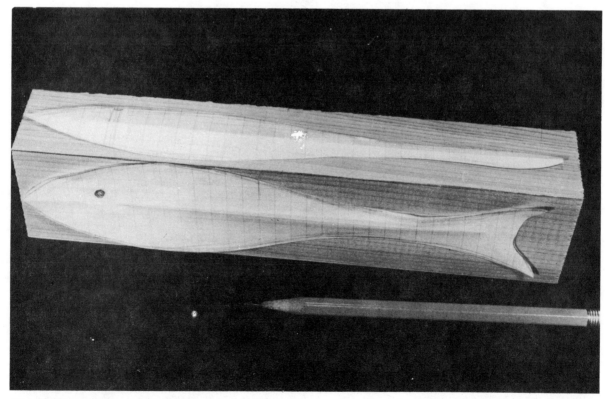

Illus. 338. Transfer patterns to the top and side surfaces.

Illus. 339. Saw the top-view shape first.

Illus. 340. Tape all the cuttings back together and cut out the side profile shape.

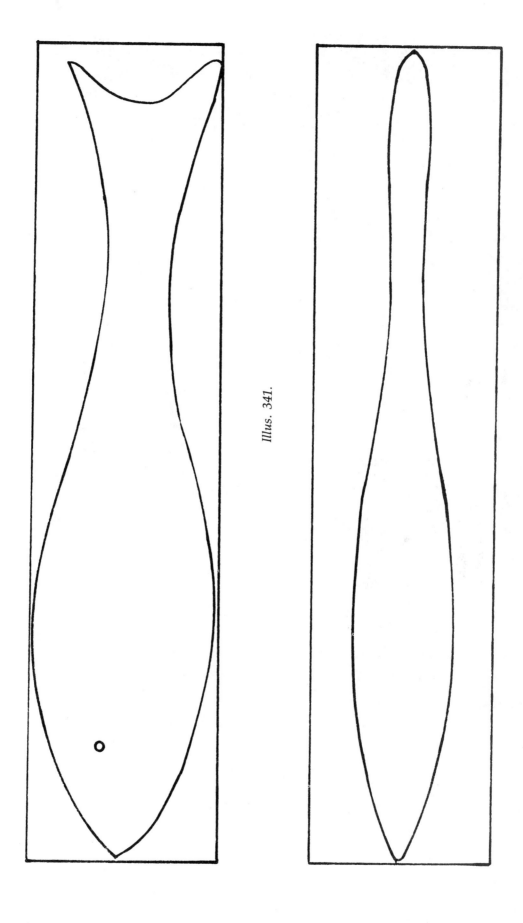

Illus. 341.

Illus. 342. Compound-sawn tulip.

Illus. 343. This weed holder and wood candle were made when a heart design was compound-sawn through. This candle is the replacement type used in food warmers that comes in a 1½-inch-diameter metal cup that's ¾ inch high.

INDEX